trinny&susannah

THE BODY SHAPE BIBLE

trinny& susannah

THE BODY SHAPE BIBLE

Forget your size Discover your shape Transform yourself

TRINNY WOODALL &
SUSANNAH CONSTANTINE

Photography by Robin Matthews

WEIDENFELD & NICOLSON

This 2008 hardback edition produced exclusively for WHSmith PLC
First published in Great Britain
in 2007 by Weidenfeld & Nicolson
10 9 8 7 6 5 4 3 2 1

The Orion Publishing Group's policy is to use papers that are natural, renewable and recyclable
products and made from wood grown in sustainable forests. The logging and manufacturing
processes are expected to conform to the environmental regulations of the country of origin.

Design director David Rowley
Editorial director Susan Haynes
Designed by Clive Hayball
Assisted by Justin Hunt and Tony Chung
Edited by Jinny Johnson
Picture research by Joanna Cannon

Printed in Italy

Weidenfeld & Nicolson
The Orion Publishing Group Ltd
Orion House
5 Upper St Martin's Lane
London WC2H 9EA
www.orionbooks.co.uk

An Hachette Livre Company

Contents

Read this first
IT'S SHAPE THAT MATTERS, NOT SIZE

WHEN WE WROTE *What Not to Wear*, we focused on the body flaws that we had found women were most unhappy about. We advised, in a very simple way, how to show off what you loved and hide what you loathed about your body.

In doing so, we inadvertently caused a mini revolution. It was exciting to see how a bit of attention paid to a few dodgy areas prodded women to set out on a path, via clothes, to self-confidence. We had hit a nerve, and might easily have downed tools there, leaving you with a few morsels of sensible advice that helped flatter a big boob here and minimise a saddlebag there.

Were it not for you continuing to air other frustrations, and asking us what to do when fixing one flaw seemed to play up another, we would not have been spurred on to keep developing and refining our method until we arrived at this totally new concept in dressing women.

The Body Shape Bible is the result of thirteen years of assessing and dressing women of all shapes, sizes and ages, and realising quite simply that shape is the single most important factor in influencing how you dress. This is the definitive guide to understanding your shape, and therefore how best to dress it.

How to feel good about yourself
Now if you are a woman who has a trim, fit, 34-24-34 figure with pert breasts, a high, round butt, silky skin and the legs of a racehorse, back away from this book now. You are in an atom-sized minority who will look divine in sacking and sandals with socks.

This is not a book about how to ice the cup cake of perfection. Rather it is about how to create a fabulous confection from what you've already got.

As a pair of imperfectionistas ourselves, we have never advocated perfection in a womanly form. We believe inner confidence radiates beauty and that confidence comes from knowing you look great – so it's a bit of a Catch 22 situation.

While we have no absolute definition of what is beautiful in the eye of the beholder, we have found that most women are agreed on what does not look good: hunched shoulders, tummy rolls hanging over jeans, boobs around the waist, flabby upper arms… to mention but a few.

Equally, Barbie doll flawlessness brings out envy and resentment from the inadequate club. Look at the relief we feel when we see poor Cameron's spot or Angelina's cellulite spring forth from the pages of a gossip weekly.

So how are women supposed to feel good about themselves?

Many of us just give in to the impossibility of looking fabulous. And that is what we have to fight. We have to fight against a mass resignation to becoming invisible. It's so wrong that a woman should disappear just because she hates her bottom, boobs or tummy. It's galling to find out that a woman has put her life on hold because her zip won't do up any more. It is heartbreaking to discover that women don't look their best because they think they can't or are just not worth it.

So often we come across women who are simply unable to see their attributes because they are so confused by their own bodies. As we have said, isolating individual faults helped immensely, but it did not provide the complete solution. No woman is the possessor of only one flaw or asset. We are made up of many.

Women's bodies are as individual as snowflakes

The premise for *The Body Shape Bible* came from you and your queries: *'My top half is neat, but I hate my big bum and thighs'* (you're a Skittle), *'Whatever I wear, I always feel big'* (read the Cello), *'My tummy dictates how I dress'* (we have great tips for Apples). *'My body is like a boy's. I find it difficult to look feminine'* (read our advice for the Cornet). *'I feel most uncomfortable wearing a swimsuit because of my saddlebags and chunky calves'* (you are a Pear), *'With my shape, I always play it safe'* (reading the Column should sort you out), *'I'm really big up top, but people admire my legs'* (then you must be a Goblet), *'My bum is wider than my shoulders. I can never find a dress to fit'* (read the Bell), *'My boobs direct the way I dress'* (the classic Hourglass). *'I've got enormous knockers, and life was difficult growing up, but I've learned to live with them'* (give thanks, you're a Lollipop), *'I know I have a shape somewhere, but I can't seem to find it'* (don't worry, a Brick can look so glamorous) or *'People find my figure sexy, but I sometimes just feel frumpy'* (that's because you're a Vase).

The fact is that women's bodies are as individual as snowflakes, yet we all share attributes and problems. Over and over again, women were asking advice on a whole range of issues. The penny finally dropped. We realised that the traditional definitions of Pear, Apple, Hourglass and Triangle were too limiting. So we embarked on a period of intensive study and research to see where this realisation would take us. We broke down, pulled apart, inspected, dissected and finally re-classified the thousands of women's bodies we have come across into twelve definitive female shapes.

Which body shape are you?

The new categories cover the most common fusions of the female form. Ninety-nine per cent of women will fall into one (or possibly two) of these categories. You may not think you have good legs or a small waist. Indeed, you will very likely think you are too fat, too thin, too tall or too small to fall into any one of these classifications. You might even have found that your shape morphed after childbirth or the menopause.

TRINNY: *'I am a skinny Pear. Mel, who has been photographed in this book, is a medium Pear. Even if you are a larger Pear, you will suit the same clothes as both of us.'*

SUSANNAH: *'I am a typical Vase – big tits with hips that balance my top half, and a gently defined waist. I know to keep it simple and go for tailored looks which play up my curves.'*

To help you identify your shape on the next page, we have listed the main physical characteristics. Don't disqualify yourself from a shape because you don't think every one of the listed characteristics applies to you. Consider your overall silhouette.

We iterate once again, *The Body Shape Bible* is not about size. An Hourglass can just as easily be a size 8 as she can be a size 18. That is what is so maddening about shopping. So often things don't fit. This is because retailers don't take into account that a woman might be a size 16 because of her bum, her boobs or her thighs. So when we suggest ideal clothes for our twelve body types, we are not saying what size they ought to be, but which shape.

Look at the chart on the next page for an overview of the twelve shapes. Once you have detected the one which best describes you, turn to that chapter to read the defining features of your shape, and how to make the most of them. If you feel that your shape falls between two silhouettes, then read them both.

If you are uncertain, you might like to take a photo of yourself in a leotard, as we have done with the women in the book, and place your silhouette over the shapes in the book until you find the right one.

If you are still finding it difficult to pigeonhole yourself, it will help to get a bunch of friends over and turn the process into a party. Your mates will be able to look at you more objectively than you can yourself.

Once your eye and brain become accustomed to the new shapes, you will, like us, be able to spot a Cello, a Skittle, a Bell or a Lollipop at fifty paces.

To begin with, however, forget everyone else. Get to know the new you. Treat her with the love and respect she deserves. She is just as beautiful as the next person, and can be every bit as stylish in her dress and confident in her person as those women we have chosen to inspire you.

WHICH BODY SHAPE ARE YOU?

COLUMN

Shoulder width
same as hip width

Slight waist

Longer legs

LOLLIPOP

Big tits

Slight waist

Slim hips

Long legs

CORNET

Broad shoulders

Small boobs

No waist

Slim hips

Long, slim legs

VASE

Big tits

Gently curving
longer waist

Hips equal tits

Slim thighs and legs

HOURGLASS

Big tits

Small waist

Short waist

Big hips

Generous thighs

CELLO

Big boobs

Short waist

Big hips

Big bottom

Big thighs

Slim lower legs

GOBLET
Broad shoulders
Big boobs
No waist
Narrow hips
Long legs

BRICK
Broad shoulders
No waist
Average tummy
Flat bum
Chunky thighs
Chunky calves

APPLE
Average tits
Tummy bigger than tits
Quite flat bum
OK legs

SKITTLE
Average tits
Slim waist
OK tummy
Big thighs
Chunky calves

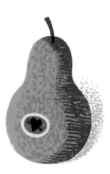

PEAR
Small tits
Long waist
Flat tummy
Saddlebags
Heavy legs

BELL
Small shoulders
Small tits
Small waist
Short waist
Big thighs
Big bottom

How we learned
TO DRESS FOR
OUR BODY SHAPE

SO YOU THINK we came out of our mothers' wombs attached by a designer umbilical cord? You might assume that because we look relatively presentable in our mid-life our earlier years must have been a breeze, free of style mistakes. Well, think again. Life was not always such a pretty picture of perfectly suited outfits for our shapes. A decade and half ago we weren't equipped to realise that Susannah's arms looked like hams in tight, elasticated sleeves or that Trinny's legs looked like stumps when cannibalised in cropped trousers.

We wore clothes that we could afford and which were in keeping with the times, thus enabling us to fit in with the crowd. And you know what? We thought we looked pretty damn great. Trinny couldn't quite see the orangeness of her fake tan. Susannah was quite happy wearing the whole-third-world-bazaar look. Ugh! All those spots, stripes and dangling coins. Seeing these pictures with educated eyes we groan with shame.

What was lacking? Why were we dressing so diabolically? The missing element was an objective eye. And the ability to look at our bodies and dress them in proportion and according to our body shapes.

It might be that you look at some of the outfits in the following pages and not like them, but you will probably agree that they work for us... because eventually we learned our body shapes and how to dress them.

The Best and the Worst

Trinny

The shape, length and colour of this dress are all great for me. It shows off my toned arms and completely covers my saddlebags. The rich fuchsia colour lifts my face if I'm feeling tired. I do revere a high heel and this sturdy shape supports the size of my leg. I also find it works really well for me to choose a colour of shoe that tones rather than contrasts with my skin tone. The less there is to break up my legs, the longer they seem.

Trinny

I loved the colour of this hat but failed to consider that it did not suit the shape of my face, only increasing the dark circles under my eyes. I must have known something was amiss because I tried to distract everyone's attention by adding that necklace-choker thing, setting up a fight with the big rose and the pattern in my dress. This is over-accessorisation at its worst.

Susannah

Having a foot injury does not excuse my wearing a high-necked, horizontal-striped Breton shirt. It makes my chest look as wide as *la Manche*.

Susannah

A tailored dress reinforced with extra-strong stretch acts as a giant corset holding all my wobbly bits in check. The wide, square neckline gives room for my cleavage to be a gentle hollow as opposed to a deep, crêpey ravine.

Trinny wrong

X Left: Having just had a baby is no excuse for my choosing shoes that are just plain wrong. The slender heel and pointed, narrow toe highlight the chunkiness of my calves and ankles made even heftier by nine months of water retention. On the plus side, I would say that this is a fabulous post-pregnancy dress. The bow draws attention to my newly enhanced bosom while soft gathers at the middle disguise any wobbliness around my tum. The gently flared skirt swishes over baby-expanded hips and thighs.

X Above: There's nothing wrong with this dress, except that it is totally wrong for my body shape. The scooped and gathered neckline would look fabulous on Susannah, but it makes my chest look like a sadly deflated balloon. I'm proud of the fact that I manage to work out and stay toned, but on reflection I think I might also be a little bit too o-l-d to be showing off quite so much stomach. I think you can tell by the look on my face that I slightly wish I'd stayed at home that night.

X Left: What was I thinking? I turned a chic gown into a fancy dress outfit with this mad hairdo. It was one of those moments when we think that a special occasion requires a special and OTT 'do'. Thank heavens I've since learned to keep it simple.

Trinny right

✓ Below: When I was pregnant I got the chance to totally re-evaluate my good points. It was wonderful choosing clothes to show off my lovely new bosom and glowing face – and hide absolutely everything else.

✓ Left: With this look I've learned how to soften my boyish torso by wearing a feminine chiffon shirt with a pussy bow underneath the more severe dress.

✓ Left: This dress succeeds fabulously where the yellow one (opposite page) failed so miserably. The striking fretwork of chiffon and crystals reveals enough skin on my top half to be eye-catchingly sexy without being obviously slutty. This is a great example of how to turn a flat chest into a positive asset. Women with bigger tits would not be able to get away with such a revealing style.

✓ Above: This is one of THE best outfits for my body, using the elements of shape, colour, texture and pattern. The textured gilet broadens out my top half, balancing saddlebags below. The slinky vest shows off my skinny midriff and the floor length skirt covers my hips and thighs, at the same time hiding a pair of killer heels designed to maximise my leg length. Big, dangly earrings make my long neck appear positively swan-like. Keeping the outfit all in tones of one colour allows me to use a patterned skirt in slinky fabric to feminise what might otherwise be a slightly severe look.

Susannah wrong

✗ Right: Here we see too much of a good thing gone very wrong indeed. The fur, sequins, messy hair... it's all too much. My big boobs cannot take such a bulky collar and why on earth have I hidden my best assets – my legs and ass?

✗ Above: We are the world. Mixing patterns, textures and jewels can be great when done with finesse, but here I took the United Nations approach with each part of my body representing a different country.

✗ Above: This could have worked so fabulously, but it didn't. The dress is perfect for my boobs with the bare shoulders making my arms look thinner, but the choker – it's so aptly named. My short little neck is being strangled by leather and metal... I really should keep my sex life under wraps. And as for that HAIR! Gelled up like a transexual Tintin – with roots.

✗ Above: Scarier than the hair and make-up is the polo neck. Just look at the way it has scrambled my tits into one lumpy mass of over-cooked eggs.

Susannah right

✓ Left: This dress is a great length to show off my legs to their shapliest. I'm lucky that my legs can cope with ankle straps. What I love the most though is the ruched bodice that hides my fat tum.

✓ Left: I was five months pregnant in this picture. What disguises the fact is that I am wearing a tiny jacket which is holding it all together.

✓ Right: This fabulous dress follows all our rules. A deep V neckline reduces tit size while great detail at the shoulder distracts attention away from my chest and also helps to slim my arm with a slicing effect. A tight band emphasises my waist and the sculptured skirt makes my legs look so long. I love it.

✓ Right: I chalk this look up as a success. Slim trousers look fab on my skinny legs and the wrap top does great things to my bust and waist. Big balloony cuffs are another way to emphasise the waist and wearing one colour extends the length of my overall silhouette.

✓ Left: This is my dress from heaven. The sweetheart neckline frames my boobs, my wrinkly upper arms are hidden and feminised by the puff sleeve whilst the tight skirt clings to my bum and thighs, which are definitely the slimmest part of my body.

The Twelve Definitive Women's Body Shapes

The Skittle
The Goblet
The Hourglass
The Cornet
The Cello
The Apple
The Column
The Bell
The Vase
The Brick
The Lollipop
The Pear

The Skittle

'My top half is neat, but I hate my big bum and thighs'

Average tits

Slim waist

OK tummy

Big thighs

Chunky calves

The Skittle
YOUR SHAPE

WE'VE CHRISTENED YOU The Skittle. You know, the old-fashioned sort that has a long, slim top half which widens dramatically at the bottom. You are not the classic Pear. She has saddlebags and a big bum. With you the problem lies further down – it's a thigh situation.

You have been broadcasting the bad news about your thighs for so long now that you're convinced that is all anyone ever notices about you. Covering them up has become your obsession. In your desperation to hide those thighs you have obliterated your entire body. Gone are your shapely arms. Gone is your little waist. Gone are your nicely turned ankles. All your best features have been forced into chin-to-toe fabric that leaves no possibility of those thighs being noticed by anyone, even yourself.

Interestingly, a larger lower half is so much easier to disguise than a bulky bust or billowing belly. Skinnier torsos allow for elegant garments that have no need to hide any lumps or bumps, and generally speaking one's bottom and thighs spend more time concealed beneath tables, steering wheels or blankets than the upper body parts.

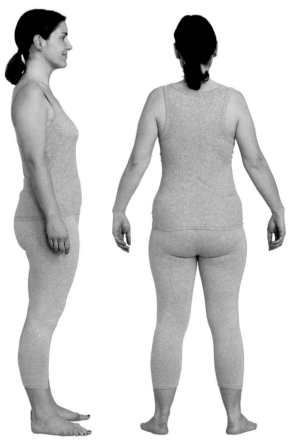

'WITH YOU, THE PROBLEM LIES FURTHER DOWN – IT'S A THIGH SITUATION'

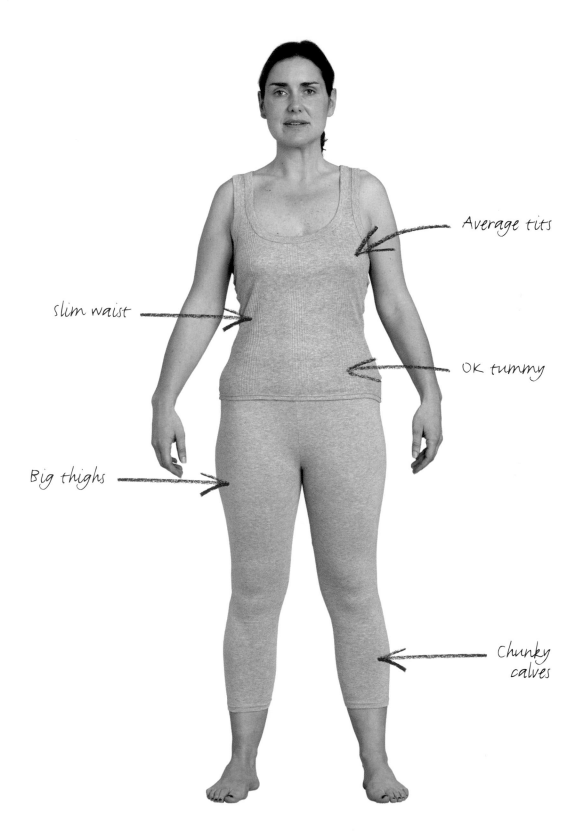

Average tits

slim waist

OK tummy

Big thighs

Chunky
calves

The Skittle

YOUR BIGGEST MISTAKES

YOUR SHAPE IS ALL FEMALE. Unfortunately, you are so mortified by the sight of your thighs that you have decided to do everything in your power to hide your entire body from the world.

The bagginess of this jumper completely diminishes your breasts. Your short neck is swamped by the huge polo neck, and your tiddly little heart-on-a-chain necklace is lost in a sea of chunky knit. The purpose of jewellery is to draw the eye to a particularly desirable part of your gorgeous body. Can you honestly say that your sexiest body part is your woolly upper chest?

You have a long body and relatively short legs so choosing a long jumper and short trousers is possibly the biggest mistake you can make. You have effectively halved the length of your legs. The stretch fabric of these trousers emphasises every bulge around the thighs giving a distinctly porcine appearance to your upper leg.

And then, you have under-pinned everything with a spindly heel, lending a teetering feel to your overall look.

Never wear

Spaghetti-strap tops
Jackets that cut across the bum
Cropped trousers
Stretch trousers of any style
Calf-length straight skirts
Pencil skirts
Ankle straps

'CHOOSING A LONG JUMPER AND SHORT TROUSERS IS POSSIBLY THE BIGGEST MISTAKE YOU CAN MAKE'

The Skittle
KEY SHAPES

Shirt
The bow detail on this shirt draws attention upwards to your tits. The puff sleeves broaden your shoulders to balance your big thighs.

Skirt
The stiff fabric and panelling holds in everything around your hips and the shape then flares over your upper legs. Any vertical pattern on your bottom half will help to slim the appearance of your thighs.

Dress
This is your dream dress. It clings in all the right places on your top half and the skinny belt accentuates your tiny waist. The skirt then drapes outwards, drawing a discreet veil over the width of your thighs. The swishy movement of shiny fabric is ultra-feminine.

Jacket
Big lapels and a wide-cut neckline serve to broaden the appearance of your shoulders, balancing your bottom half. A cropped jacket gives the illusion of lengthening your legs and it's sufficiently hugging to enhance your little waist.

Top
Draping sleeves slim the arms and the body-hugging fabric shows the shape of your slim waist. Wearing a bit of colour and glitter as shown in this purple top attracts attention to your trim and shapely top half.

Coat
This coat follows the same principles as your jacket. Broad lapels draw the eye to your shoulders and show a shapely torso. The coat then flares to the knee, covering the bulge of your thighs.

Jumper
Worn over a feminine blouse, this fitted knit moulds to your figure and gives a curvy shape.

Trousers
Wide-leg, flat-front trousers that hang from the top of your bum won't cling to your thighs. The pockets are at an angle, rather than on the side seam, so they won't pull and appear to be straining. Wearing a darker colour on your lower half will help to slim the legs.

Swimsuit
Your problem area is your thigh, rather than saddlebags, so a lower cut leg balances the width in your upper leg. Expose as much shoulder as possible to draw the eye upward. The big buckle between your breasts concentrates attention in just the right place.

Shoes
Because your legs are short you want a high, high heel. A spindly stiletto would be completely out of balance with your legs. These chunky heels are just perfect.

Big bow blouse

Vertically panelled skirt

Clingy dress with flared skirt

Broad lapel cropped jacket

Body-hugging sparkly top

Fitted coat with flared skirt

Fitted knit

High chunky heel

Wide-leg trousers with pockets on an angle

Low-leg swimsuit with big buckle at breast

The Skittle
YOUR BEST LOOK
CASUAL

BEHIND ALL THE OUTFITS we will show you are principles concerned with lessening the appearance of your thighs, lengthening your legs and focusing attention on your shapely torso. If you only ever own one pair of trousers, let these be the ones: flat-fronted and wide-legged, this trouser falls straight to the floor from the widest point of your butt. This is the only way to allow maximum roominess for the leg without the trouser becoming a baggy garment.
It is absolutely vital that the cloth does not cling to your legs at any point.

The colour should be one of the darker shades of your palette. Charcoal grey and dark brown are most versatile, closely followed by dark blue. Contrary to popular belief, black trousers are not the most useful. It is quite difficult to team black with other tones apart from more black, and a head-to-toe black look can look exceedingly drab unless the quality and cut are exquisite. Besides, this is about creating a casual daytime look, not funeral attire.

A fabric that has some weight to it will hold its shape better than anything that stretches or drapes. This is really helpful in obscuring any bulkiness beneath the surface. Check where the pockets are. If they are on an angle at the hip that's fine, but if they're in the side seam of the trouser they will pull and strain.

Your legs are short in proportion to your body so we want to do everything possible to stretch them. This doesn't mean you have to wear six-inch heels to walk the dog. Everyone needs a pair of comfortable trainers, but always make sure your trouser legs fall all the way to the heel of your shoe. Your second pair of trousers can be an even longer pair for wearing with heels on smarter occasions.

Having done as much as possible to conceal your lower section we now want to throw a spotlight on your trim, tasty top half. Adding a little colour and shimmer will lift your look. And there is no need to be afraid of clingy fabrics. They will show off the pleasing smallness of your waist.

A medium-weight, knee-length coat will be one of your best friends for at least half the year so choose it well. The coat should fit snugly around your bust and waist and then flare to the knee, completely covering your nether regions.

'A MEDIUM-WEIGHT, KNEE-LENGTH COAT WILL BE ONE OF YOUR BEST FRIENDS FOR AT LEAST HALF THE YEAR SO CHOOSE IT WELL...'

The Skittle
YOUR BEST LOOK
SMART

WHAT? EXPOSE MY LEGS? During the daytime? Wearing a dress during the day is as revolutionary to your mind as popping out for a bit of Bastille-storming. The art of illusion is based not on total cover-up. Rather it's the subtle skill of creating a different impression – the one you want people to have.

Whether it's in the office, the boardroom or on the social battlefield of life, looking feminine is one of the key weapons in a woman's armory. Wearing trousers to every possible occasion depletes your femininity. And it's just boring. We want to show you how to choose the right dress that will make you feel like a gracious swan rather than an ungainly duckling.

As with the previous casual outfit, the body of this dress is fitted to make the most of your svelte top half. Your shoulders are not the narrowest of all the women in this book, but it is a good strategy to broaden your upper body whenever possible so that it appears balanced with the bottom. Wearing a wide-cut neckline with outward pointing lapels will achieve this effect.

A slim waist is an enviable asset so why not show it off with a skinny belt? Not everyone can wear these – you can, so do it.

The cut of this dress is actually quite conservative but, as with your sparkly top, the shiny fabric adds a bit of pizzazz. Look for a skirt that won't cling to your thighs, but will swish around your legs when you walk. Anything that serves to create vertical lines on your bottom half is really helpful, so the fact that this dress falls in soft folds from the hip is an added point in its favour.

Make sure that the hemline falls on your knee, never above it. It will feel scary to you to skim so dangerously close to exposing your thighs, but we want to reassure you that, at this length, a full skirt will elegantly veil the excess flesh that lurks beneath. Chunky calves can be made to look shapelier by wearing fine mesh fishnet tights.

So, next time you are called to attend an important business meeting or a smart lunch you can bin the trousers and step forth with a new feminine confidence.

'A SLIM WAIST IS AN ENVIABLE ASSET... NOT EVERYONE CAN WEAR A SKINNY BELT – YOU CAN, SO DO IT'

The Skittle
YOUR BEST LOOK
PARTY

NOW THAT YOU'VE GOT the hang of feminine dressing, it's time to take it one step further. You may in the past have dipped your toe into party wear by buying a cut-on-the-bias, spaghetti-strap dress, possibly in chiffon, and then retired hurt, scurrying back to those trusty old black trousers brightened up with a vaguely festive top. Don't worry, it's happened to many women we've worked with. The fact is that those floaty, barely there dresses make you feel like a hippo in a tutu.

For your silhouette, the solution is sexy with structure. Take a look at Claire. Her bottom and thighs are tamed by a structured skirt. The skirt is fitted so it hugs and lifts the bum, yet it doesn't emphasise the width of the haunches because it flicks out at the hem, giving a balanced outline.

So far you have a flattering, but rather plain skirt. What absolutely makes this outfit is the fabulous jacket. It has enough unique details, like the off-centre buttons and shaped sleeves, to make it an attention-grabber without being fussy in any way. The cut sculpts your body to perfection, pulling in your waist, pushing up your breasts and giving you the curvaceous poise of a Plantaganet princess. If you really want to work it to the max, make sure you lift your bum and tits high, high, high with magic knickers and a gel bra.

The diamond-shaped neckline is one of the best for broadening the appearance of your chest, again balancing your bottom half.

This is an outfit where all the drama is created by the cut, rather than sequins, beads and ribbons. The secret to pulling it off with panache is to keep it simple.

The only decorations you will need are killer shoes, fabulous earrings and an immaculate hairstyle.

'THE CUT SCULPTS
YOUR BODY TO
PERFECTION,
PULLING IN
YOUR WAIST,
PUSHING UP
YOUR BREASTS
AND GIVING YOU
THE CURVACEOUS
POISE OF A
PLANTAGANET
PRINCESS'

WHAT IT MEANS
TO BE A SKITTLE

∗ You need a pair of very well-cut trousers and that's a hard thing to find. Good tailoring is always more expensive, so start saving up. Try Max Mara, Nicole Farhi, Giorgio Armani or Wallis. Remember that cheap trousers are a false economy for you. You'll get more wear out of a pair that fit you beautifully. The simple equation is: number of times worn ÷ price = real cost.

∗ By constantly telling yourself that you hate your thighs you are sending yourself such negative messages that eventually your thighs are only thing that you will see. The power of positive thought cannot be underestimated. Here is an affirmation for you: 'I love my body and my tiny waist and now I know how to dress to disguise my thighs, I don't mind them at all.'

∗ If you exercise, it is vital that you spend as much time stretching as you do training. You are susceptible to building up muscles that will enlarge your thighs. Stretching elongates the muscles.

∗ You have often bought trousers that fit on the thigh and then compromised your waist shape by covering the gape with loose tops. Rather than throw all those trousers away, find a good dressmaker and have them all taken in at the waist.

★ Although you are wildly self-conscious about your rear end, most people will focus on your face and top half. Give thanks that we spend most of our lives sitting down (on first dates, at work, at a dinner party) and that you have a great top half.

★ For your perfect photo: stand with one hand on your hip and the other over one thigh to break up its width. Then drop the hip of that thigh to create a sexy shape.

'REMEMBER THAT... YOU HAVE A GREAT TOP HALF'

SKITTLES
TO INSPIRE YOU...

Halle Berry

✓ Look what clever Halle Berry has done. She's donned a dress that does everything to enhance her slim waist and torso. The flared sleeves end just at the waist so further focusing our gaze in that spot while the skirt drapes her thighs and gives a lovely swishy movement when she walks. Low-cut nude shoes extend her legs as much as possible.

✗ Rule one for a Skittle: never wear skinny jeans. Rule two for a Skittle: never wear skinny jeans. Rule three for a Skittle...

Sharon Osbourne

✓ Sharon Osbourne is a woman who has reversed the flow of time. She dresses so appropriately for her age, still managing to look sexy without looking silly. Her makeup isn't stuck in a 1980s rock-chick time warp. There's plenty of it but it's applied with the skill and sophistication of the woman herself.

Sharon has learned to keep her legs covered. Wide-legged trousers skim the thighs while the very fitted jacket throws the spotlight on her top half. Long fitted sleeves really work to slim her silhouette and, as we well know, wearing all one colour lengthens her all over.

✗ This big baggy cardie does nothing to enhance Sharon's neat upper body. To be honest, she may as well have just worn a horse blanket. The way it sticks out at the bottom says 'Hey, look at my arse.' Just in case you might miss it, the knitter has added some coloured stripes to point the way.

Meryl Streep

✓ This look is just sensational for making the most of a Skittle silhouette. The fitted top encircles Meryl's little waist and then the neckline widens into a dramatic trapeze, adding breadth to her top half and at the same time showing off her neat breasts. As for hiding the thighs, the super extravagant skirt does a brilliant job. For all we know she could be hiding a double-decker bus under that skirt.

✗ Remember those trousers we said you should never wear? Well, Meryl is wearing them here. Tapered and short, they make her legs seem like stumpy pegs. The shapeless shirt does nothing to avert our gaze from the width of her lower regions. It's no wonder she's coyly trying to cover up with a big lacy hat.

The Goblet

'I'm really big up top, but people admire my legs'

Broad shoulders

Big boobs

No waist

Narrow hips

Long legs

The Goblet
YOUR SHAPE

LOOKING AT YOUR SILHOUETTE a classic crystal goblet springs to mind. We see a shape that is heavy and square above, balanced on an elegant, slender stem.

With you the trouble is at the top. Yes, you are the bearer of large breasts, a generous tummy and a broad back to support your ample front. But, hey, look at those legs. Those are what we need to focus on because they were born for fishnets and sexy high heels.

Feeling fabulous is all about making those pins even longer than they already are. You can glide into most trousers and will be able to show off your limbs well into old age for they are the last things to go on a woman.

A shapely ankle lasts almost as long as a diamond heirloom – and we would argue it's probably more valuable.

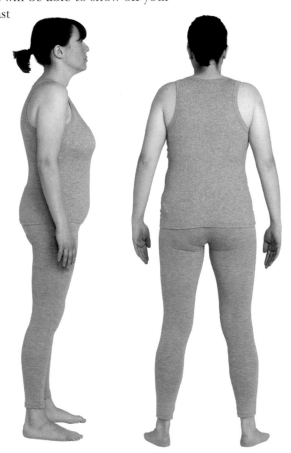

'WE SEE A SHAPE THAT IS HEAVY AND SQUARE ABOVE, BALANCED ON AN ELEGANT, SLENDER STEM'

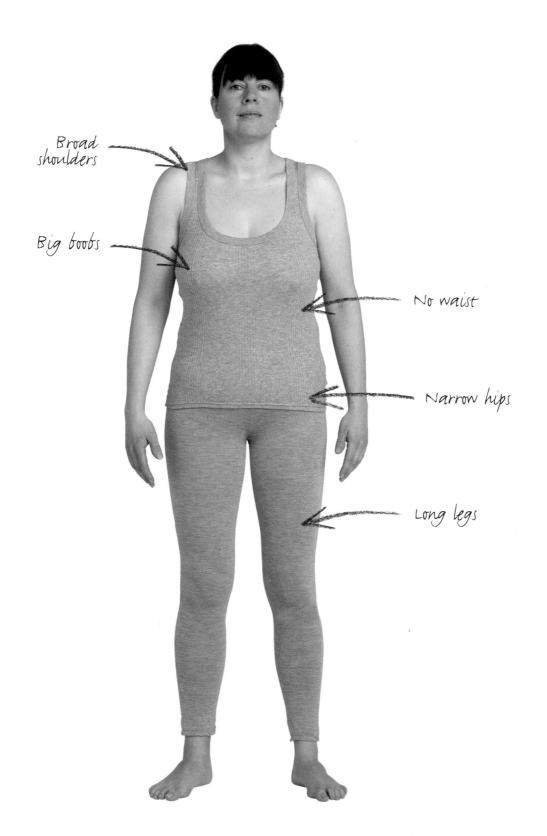

Broad shoulders

Big boobs

No waist

Narrow hips

Long legs

The Goblet
YOUR BIGGEST MISTAKES

THE SQUARE CUT of your body is vastly exaggerated by this boxy, shapeless shift. From the front, back or side, it's all the same, and we are hard pushed to realise you have two breasts, rather than just one big cushion stuffed down your front. And your waist is completely erased. From shoulders to hemline, it makes you look like a large cardboard box.

While trying to make the best of a bad job, you are showing off your lovely legs – by wearing the dress short with stand-out tights. But the contrast of colours between your legs and torso makes you look top heavy, like a big billboard nailed to a post. Wearing the brightest colour on your body only adds to the effect.

The slashed neckline broadens your swimmer's shoulders and increases the area of your chest. Your jewellery is not chosen to suit your shape – it's just the jewellery that you wear every day, with every outfit.

Heavy, square-heeled shoes are not only dull, they are also too clumpy for your legs, and make them appear spindly rather than shapely.

Never wear

Wide-legged sweat pants

Shift dresses

Chunky knit sweaters

Slashed necklines

Double-breasted jackets

Skinny belts

'FROM THE FRONT, BACK OR SIDE, IT'S ALL THE SAME... AND YOUR WAIST IS COMPLETELY ERASED'

The Goblet
KEY SHAPES

Top

The deep wide V neckline halves the area of your chest. Always pull the top up slightly so that the fabric falls in folds over your middle, confusing the eye and disguising any unwanted folds of flesh.

Skirt

Suede (or suedette) is the most fabulous fabric for holding in a rounded tummy. The horizontal panelling further lifts and restrains the spread.

Coat

You don't naturally have a curvy waist, but you can create one with a very fitted and belted coat. The big flap pockets on the hip add even more shapeliness to your silhouette. A small check pattern breaks up the area of your top half.

Top

The trim of this empire-line fitted top extends the line of the V, further separating and lessening the size of your bosom. Add to that another trim encircling the slim part of your torso under your boobs, a flared shape to skim your tum and a small pattern to break up your top half, and you have the perfect top to flatter your shape.

Jacket

A snug, waisted jacket winches you in and creates that highly desirable hourglass outline.

Swimsuit

This is the miracle swimsuit. It lifts and separates your boobs, sucks in your tummy and creates the illusion of a waist with diagonal gathers. The wide set of the straps also helps to narrow your shoulders.

Skirt

A skirt that is fitted at the top strokes those svelte legs while the flaring hemline balances out your top half.

Jeans

Resist the urge to wear baggy trousers to cover your bulging belly. Instead show off the luxurious length of your legs with slimline jeans. Always make sure the waistline is low cut and your tummy is covered with a longer top.

Dress

This dress does everything in its power to reduce the size of your knockers, cover your tum and concentrate attention on the slimmest section of torso under your bust. If your upper arms are a bit wobbly, the balloon sleeves kindly draw the eye to your slimmer forearm.

Shoes

Although your legs are wonderfully long and slender, a very thin heel would emphasise your top-heaviness. These heels are curvy enough to complement your shapely leg, yet still have some solidity to give you balance.

Deep wide - neck top

Panelled skirt in heavy fabric

**Single-breasted coat
with big pockets**

Empire-line fitted top

Fitted short jacket

Miracle swimsuit

Tight skirt with fluted hemline

Curvy, yet sturdy, heels

Low-waisted, slimline jeans

Scoop neck, balloon-sleeved dress

The Goblet
YOUR BEST LOOK
CASUAL

THE AIM OF ALL your outfits is to strike a balance between your relative chunkiness above and your slim shapeliness below.

Drop-dead gorgeous legs are the perfect filling for slim-fitting jeans. The vast majority of your sisters with big thighs, butts and saddlebags can never sport this sexy style so count yourself blessed indeed. You can either dress them down with trainers or up with heels.

Exaggerating the gazelle-like proportions of your legs leaves us with a new problem to tackle – how to keep the look of your top half in proportion and minimise your top heaviness. Firstly, we need to manage those breasts by lifting and separating. Any kind of cross-over or wrap top will do nicely. A top that then hugs you under your boobs as well does double duty because it also creates that all-important slimming band at the narrowest part of your torso.

As an example of her worst possible look, Annabel wore a shift dress in one solid colour. This made her top half look like a sail unfurled in the wind. Learning how to use texture and pattern to break up your body is key for you. Here a small busy print on her top does the trick of sending our eyes travelling in many different directions, confusing us to the point that we pay no notice to any outline of tummy or sturdiness of waist hiding beneath the surface. The decorative trim on the bust draws our attention to how up and apart her boobs are and to how small the circumference of her torso is.

A three-quarter length coat ties your casual outfits together. For you, it is a must-have garment that will be used on all but the hottest days of the year. Look for a coat that has a smallish check or pattern and a definite waist to it. Make sure that it is single breasted – so as not to broaden your chest.

'LEARNING
HOW TO USE
TEXTURE AND
PATTERN TO
BREAK UP YOUR
BODY IS KEY
FOR YOU'

The Goblet
YOUR BEST LOOK
SMART

A DEEP V NECKLINE serves two purposes. It breaks up the expanse of your chest and it extends the line of your neck by several inches. You can vary the look by wearing a lighter coloured vest beneath when you're feeling modest, or without when you're in the mood to flash a bit of train-stopping cleavage.

As with practice of the ancient Japanese art of origami, real skill is required for t-shirt arranging. When wearing a clingy top, always make sure that it is long enough to fall into a few drapes across your middle. Never, ever, pull your top tightly down over your midriff. If you find that this is a habit, of yours, practise instead pulling your top up slightly in moments of nervous distraction and then nimbly arranging it in a few soft folds with your fingertips.

This is a smart look for lunch or a meeting so you'll want a jacket. No doubt you have some sort of puffa for walking the dog, although if you've been travelling with us on our journey up to now we trust that you have long since consigned it to the garden shed. Just stop and think before you top off your new look with your old shapeless jacket. Do you really want to revert to your former billboard-nailed-to-a-post look and ruin all our hard work. No? We knew you wouldn't. So, even if it feels like donning an alien skin, we want you to ensure that your wardrobe contains at least one figure-hugging, fitted jacket that is shaped to go in at the waist. If you wear it unbuttoned, the line of the jacket will slice your torso vertically into three slimmer slivers. Wearing it buttoned will cinch in your waist, giving much-needed curviness to your silhouette.

With hips and thighs so slender, you can afford to wear a skirt made of a heavier fabric. Suede is one of the best for obliterating belly bulges. This skirt has horizontal panels that serve to flatten your abdomen. Suede skirts are expensive to buy and keep clean. Luckily, suedette does just as good a job.

We want your gorgeous legs to be the focus of all the attention. To this end, your shoes are the most important item in your ensemble. These have the sexy sheen of satin and a heel that is solid enough to balance top-heaviness. The curve of the heel reflects the elegant curve of your calf.

'WE WANT
YOUR GORGEOUS
LEGS TO BE THE
FOCUS OF ALL
THE ATTENTION.
TO THIS END,
YOUR SHOES
ARE THE MOST
IMPORTANT
ITEM IN YOUR
ENSEMBLE'

The Goblet
YOUR BEST LOOK
PARTY

THE GOLDEN RULE of tummy reduction is to find a bra that will lift and thrust forward your boobs. It's all about perception: if your tits jut outward like the prow of the Ark Royal then everything immediately below pales into insignificance. The trick is how to pull this off without frightening all the horses, so make sure that the cup size is big enough to hold your entire bosom without spill-over and that the bra straps are broad enough to smooth over any excess flab on your back.

Our next top tip for evenings and special occasions is to don a pair of bulge-flattening magic knickers. With good foundations laid, look for a dress that follows the basic principles for your body shape.

A deeply scooped neckline is fantastic for a bit of night-time spotlight on your cleavage. Unless you have been a fanatical swimmer or gymnast you probably carry some weight on your arms as well as your back and shoulders. A dress with slightly puffed long sleeves covers any looseness at the tops of your arms and saves you having to wear a shrug.

By clever use of texture alone, the swathe of ribbing on this dress creates the illusion of a contrasting, breast-reducing panel down the centre of the bust. It then metamorphoses into a slimming band under the boobs.

At all costs, avoid any floaty, diaphanous styles. They're too insubstantial for your frame. Instead, rely on heavier fabrics with added sparkle to bring a touch of evening magic to your look.

'A DEEPLY
SCOOPED
NECKLINE IS
FANTASTIC FOR
A BIT OF NIGHT-
TIME SPOTLIGHT
ON YOUR
CLEAVAGE'

WHAT IT MEANS TO BE A GOBLET

* Any female who grows up with broad shoulders and early sprouting breasts is liable to be labelled fat as a child. Your sense of size and confidence can be forever undermined by such comments. It is really important that you re-evaluate the shape you are as an adult, concentrating on all that is fabulous and womanly about your form.

* You have broad shoulders and a larger décolleté. Acknowledge your chest as one of your best assets and take care of it. Avoid submerging your bust in very hot water and always wear a high-factor sun lotion, even when you're not sunbathing.

* You are most suited to classic looks. If you want to look up-to-date, choose fashionable colours in the right tone for you, rather than trying to wear the latest shape.

* Your broad shoulders give you naturally great posture. They act as a coathanger for your magnificent breasts.

* As a Goblet, your body shape is one that is inclined to thicken at the waist when you reach menopause. Gentle yoga or Pilates classes will help.

* You have a great shape for pregnancy. Women who carry their weight on their lower half tend to suffer from water retention during pregnancy and that prevents them from wearing dresses, but you can simply take your existing stretchy dresses and just grow gently inside them.

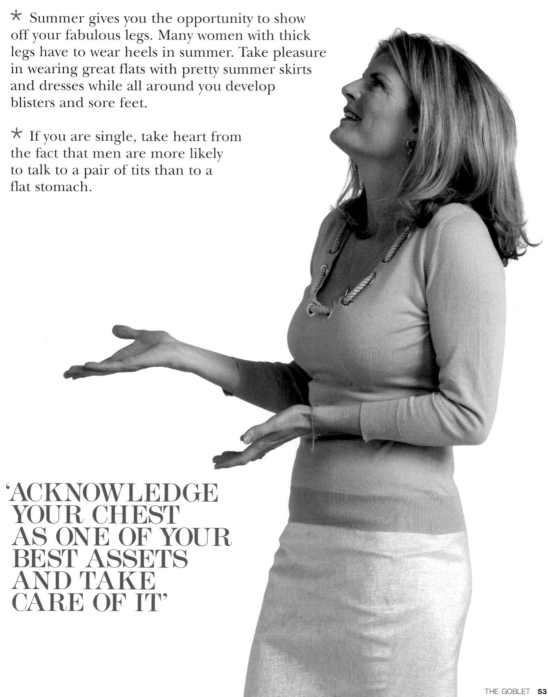

✷ Summer gives you the opportunity to show off your fabulous legs. Many women with thick legs have to wear heels in summer. Take pleasure in wearing great flats with pretty summer skirts and dresses while all around you develop blisters and sore feet.

✷ If you are single, take heart from the fact that men are more likely to talk to a pair of tits than to a flat stomach.

'ACKNOWLEDGE YOUR CHEST AS ONE OF YOUR BEST ASSETS AND TAKE CARE OF IT'

GOBLETS
TO INSPIRE YOU...

Renée Zellweger

✓ The teardrop-shaped neckline cuts a feminine curve into Renée's boxy shoulderline. Her very fitted jacket is short and shaped to give a bit of wiggle at the waist. Central buttons draw the eye inward. An archetypal pencil skirt shows dazzling legs to their utmost advantage and classic stilettos give the sexiest shape to her slim ankles.

✗ A high neckline with cutaway sleeves gives Renée's shoulders the outline of an American linebacker. It also emphasises her boobs, giving a top-heavy effect to the whole look. This shapeless shift does nothing to define her waist. It may be comfortable, but it's no friend to a square torso.

Catherine Zeta Jones

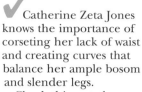

✓ Catherine Zeta Jones knows the importance of corseting her lack of waist and creating curves that balance her ample bosom and slender legs.

Check this out: the breadth of Catherine's shoulder is reduced by thick straps and further disguised by flowing hair. A black bodice shrinks her top half and then the white pattern hacks into her waist, breaking it up significantly and finally sweeping our sight line all the way down to the floor. Genius!

✗ We cannot give the Oscar for best support to this flimsy spaghetti-strap dress. It is seriously letting Catherine down. The big bold arrow pattern broadens her middle making her look much bigger than she really is and the skirt below just hangs about doing absolutely nothing.

Jessica Lange

✓ This is one of the simplest and best looks for a Goblet. Trust Jessica Lange to turn out in ultimate style. The uncluttered line of the jacket in a colour that contrasts with the dress slices her broader upper half in two. A tight-fitting, shimmery skirt allows her gorgeous legs to do all the work.

✗ Jessica is too broad up top to be messing around with fiddly prints, clingy, slithery fabric or, horror of horrors, spaghetti straps. Each of these on their own is a crime against the Goblet. Putting them all together really cannot be countenanced.

The
Hourglass

'My boobs direct the way I dress'

Big tits

Small waist

Short waist

Big hips

Generous thighs

The Hourglass
YOUR SHAPE

A PAINTER'S DREAM... that's what you are. Throughout the course of history the Hourglass figure has epitomised the female form. Your body is the very essence of what makes a woman womanly. So you are made for the boys, but you feel, not for clothes.

As a girl you could very well have bloomed early on. Your boobs will have attracted attention before you were mentally equipped to deal with the sniggering. This would have been hard and may have left a lingering shame over your buoyant figure. So rather than celebrating your iconic shape you will be left wondering how the hell to hide it from unwanted glances.

Younger Hourglasses feel frustrated at not being able to walk out of fashionable stores like Topshop armed with brimming bags of cool kit. How, for example, is a luscious figure supposed to carry off anything from Kate Moss's collection? Fashion to you is a barrier to looking trendy. You try out the smock dresses and blouson tops, but with your big boobs and short waist you feel pregnant. The key for you is not to hide any part of your body, but to show it off. You absolutely must wear fitted clothes that clasp your curves and stretch your torso. Would Marilyn Monroe have looked the sex bomb she was in frumpy, grungy gear?

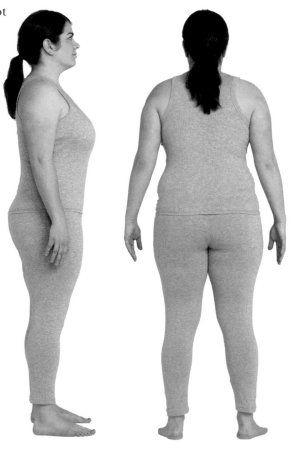

Your calling card is to strut your femininity. Think pencil skirts, fitted jackets and strapless dresses. Keep in mind the fact that most men would rather see tits and ass than a bag of bones. Keep it tight and wiggle your bum. The results will be astounding. You will no longer feel fat and lumpy.

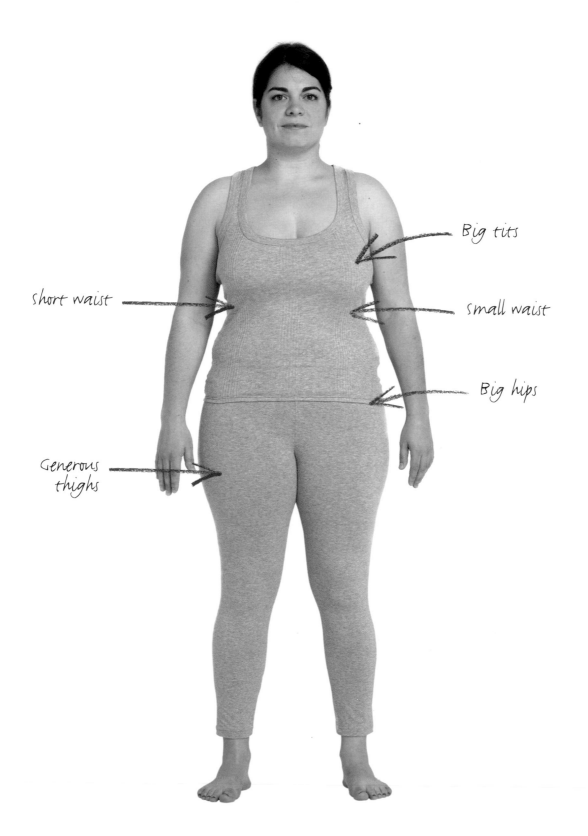

Big tits

short waist

small waist

Big hips

Generous
thighs

The Hourglass
YOUR BIGGEST MISTAKES

AS AN HOURGLASS you know you are feminine. You see that womanly figure every morning in the mirror. So it's natural to assume that this ought to be enhanced with frills, flounces, chiffon and bows. NO! These are disastrous. They turn you from burlesque beauty to blowsy barmaid in a trice.

Big decorations and excess fabric add weight and volume where it's just not needed. Take bat-wing sleeves for instance. They take your breasts on a journey that ends at the outer edge of your arms. Encasing your short waist in a wide belt will make it disappear altogether.

Flat lace-up shoes turn your legs into cloven hoofed limbs.

Never wear

Flap side pockets on trousers

Big belts

Batwing sleeves

Blouses with bows or flounces

Smocks

Flat, lace-up shoes

Ankle strap, pointy shoes

Cowboy boots

'BIG DECORATIONS AND EXCESS FABRIC ADD WEIGHT AND VOLUME WHERE IT'S JUST NOT NEEDED'

The Hourglass
KEY SHAPES

Cardigan
A deep V neck fitted cardigan is the cornerstone of every Hourglass's wardrobe. Start to build up a collection of these for summer and winter, in different colours.

Dress
Always look for a dress that lifts your boobs and elongates your waist. A small draped sleeve gives just enough coverage to your bicep. This print is about as big as your Hourglass shape can bear without being swamped.

T-shirt
Look for a t-shirt that fits your waist, is wide open at the neckline and has something to divert the eye towards your shoulders – like puffed sleeves, for example.

Trousers
It is so difficult for an Hourglass to wear trousers, the constant thigh chaffing is most off-putting. Unsightly tummy spill-over in jeans takes away from the feminine curves of your body and only makes you feel fat and uncomfortable with yourself. It can be an uphill battle, but don't despair. You can go for a drapey fabric with a stretch top. Keep the top half of your trousers hidden from prying eyes with a flattering crotch-length top.

Necklace
You don't need to over-adorn your chest, it's eye-catching enough already. A simple chain with a dangly bit that hangs below your boobs will suffice.

Pencil skirt
A pencil skirt exaggerates the curve from your hip to your knee. It is the most drop dead flattering shape for an Hourglass.

Coat
Pocket flaps on the hips emphasise your tiny nipped-in waist. The deep V plunging to your waist cuts your chest size in half.

Jacket
Two buttons sewn closely together give support and also elongate your waist. Go for a curved lapel to echo your curves. Three-quarter sleeves show off your elegant wrists and suggest a more delicate frame.

Shirt
The side fastening of this stretchy cotton shirt will give your stomach and boobs added support. Choose shirts where the buttons do not go all the way to the top, but just to the top of the boob leaving the neckline open. This will give a more flattering shape to your décolleté.

Shoes
To complement your curviness, choose cute shoes with rounded toes, peep toes or bows (pointed stilettoes are not for you).

Deep V fitted cardigan

Fitted dress that elongates the waist

Scoop-necked, fitted t-shirt with shoulder detail

Drapey trousers

Simple necklace

Pencil skirt

Deep V to nipped-in waist with full skirt and pockets on hips

Two button jacket

Side-fastening shirt with open neckline

Curvy, cute shoes

The Hourglass
YOUR BEST LOOK
CASUAL

IT IS ALWAYS DIFFICULT for an Hourglass to look convincing in weekend clothes. Your shape is just too ultra-feminine for trousers. Bear in mind that for casual occasions you must always up the ante and turn out, say, ten percent smarter than your less shapely cousins.

Your waist is short and your crotch is long. This has the effect of making you look shorter than the Vase figured woman who you are most closely related to.

The bluffer's way to longer legs is to find a top that is long enough to stop just below your crotch, thereby fooling our eyes into not knowing where your legs end and your butt begins. This top is the perfect length to wear with trousers. It does double duty by covering any squidginess in your belly while still being smart enough to complement your super-womanly shape.

'THIS TOP IS THE PERFECT LENGTH TO WEAR WITH TROUSERS... AND IT COMPLEMENTS YOUR SUPER-WOMANLY SHAPE'

The Hourglass
YOUR BEST LOOK
SMART

EVERY ITEM IN YOUR wardrobe should work to clearly define your curvy silhouette. An Hourglass needs a dress that encapsulates her figure. You need to feel that you are pouring yourself into a dress, that it is moulding to your body like a second skin. If there is an excess of loose fabric you are in the wrong dress.

This clever dress has parallel vertical seams. Like an iron, they flatten your tummy and stretch out your waist. The built-in cups help to lift your boobs away from your waist, again adding length. It is easier to have a dress taken in down the back seam than to have the bust adjusted, so make sure that your dress fits your breasts first and foremost. The broderie anglaise adds a feminine touch but the important thing is that it is a supportive fabric. This look would work equally well in flannel or wool gabardine. Avoid a fabric that is too stretchy, it will not contain your lumps and bumps. Equally, avoid lightweight silks and chiffon – they won't flatter your womanly form.

The small, neat sleeve lessens the breadth across your chest. Like most Hourglasses, Andrea has a bit of extra flesh on her upper arms so it's important that the sleeve doesn't cut into her arm. A small puff or fitted three-quarter sleeve would equally do the trick, but beware of big loose batwings or kimonos. They will merge your arms and chest into one mass of solid flesh.

Further on down, the way this dress shapes itself to your hips and bottom is a dream. It absolutely makes the most of your most enviable asset – your beautiful Hourglass shape.

'THE BRODERIE ANGLAISE ADDS A FEMININE TOUCH BUT THE IMPORTANT THING IS THAT IT IS A SUPPORTIVE FABRIC'

The Hourglass
YOUR BEST LOOK
PARTY

AS AN HOURGLASS your defining feature is your tiny waist. This doesn't necessarily mean it has to be of a twenty-inch circumference; what we mean is that your waist is tiny in comparison to your boobs and hips. So if you're a larger Hourglass (and let's face it, many of you are) your waist will be proportionately small for your size. The fact that you are short-waisted signifies two things – firstly, that you tend to look shorter than you are and, secondly, that you are likely to have a bigger tummy.

Again, it is important to stretch your body lengthwise as much as possible. Avoid obvious waistbands, belts or general slicing of the mid-torso, and look for clothes that still pinch you in at the middle.

There is nothing better than a little fitted jacket to tuck in your boobs and cuddle up to the side of your waist. The ideal way to wear this is unbuttoned with a small opening to elongate the front of your body. The inverted pleat in the middle of this dress draws our eyes to the centre of your waist and also creates an extra flick of fabric to discreetly swish over your tum.

Peep-toed shoes always look great on an Hourglass. There's something just so cute and Betty Boop sexy about them.

'YOUR WAIST IS TINY IN COMPARISON TO YOUR BOOBS AND HIPS... LOOK FOR CLOTHES THAT PINCH YOU IN AT THE MIDDLE'

WHAT IT MEANS TO BE A HOURGLASS

✱ You might feel like buckling under peer pressure to dress overly casually, but your shape looks so much better in smarter clothes. Don't be afraid to stand out.

✱ The Hourglass has been synonymous with feminine beauty through the ages so be proud to bear this label. Look to your style icons like Marilyn Monroe or Nigella Lawson and take confidence from them.

✱ At work you might not want all the attention to be on your chest. Invest in a good stock of vests to coordinate with your tops and dresses. In the evening, ditch the vest but instead use a large brooch on your shoulder to divert eyes that might otherwise spend the entire conversation glued to your cleavage.

✱ Winter presents problems. You should avoid polo necks and chunky knits... but how do you then keep your neck from freezing? Invest in fine knitted scarves that are long enough to wrap around and don't bulk you out.

✱ Don't be afraid to thrust your breasts forward in a good, supporting bra. You may feel self-conscious at first but it's a far more pleasing sight than a silhouette that is hunched over with boobs pressing downwards, creating extra belly rolls.

✱ Having that healthy layer of padding means that your skin looks younger and plumper, especially on your face and décolleté. Keep it glowing by exfoliating regularly.

✱ Make the most of the fact that all Hourglasses have a waist, a most enviable attribute that can easily be enhanced by what you choose to wear.

'THE HOURGLASS HAS BEEN SYNONYMOUS WITH FEMININE BEAUTY THROUGH THE AGES SO BE PROUD TO BEAR THIS LABEL'

HOURGLASSES TO INSPIRE YOU...

Nigella Lawson

✓ Nigella is an inspiration to all Hourglasses. She is absolutely not governed by any trend or fashion. She knows what suits her, and we would be amazed if she has a stylist. There's something always rather homemade and charming about the way she puts her clothes together. It makes her both a temptress and a mother. The cut of this dress enhances all her assets. Hugging her voluptuous hips, it exaggerates her tiny waist, hides the biggest part of her arm and shows off her Rubenesque shoulders.

✗ Wearing black from head to toe with no relief is overwhelming on an Hourglass. The long straight skirt does nothing to accentuate Nigella's gorgeous curves and a polo neck is absolutely the worst neckline for making big boobs look lumpy and unappetising. The shoulder bag is too big for a petite build.

Salma Hayek

✓ Wearing plain dark brown at the top reduces the size of Salma's boobs and a deep wide V neckline cuts them in half. Slashes of blue at the waist add to the bandaged effect and really winch her in.

✗ This dress is a mish-mash of styles and continents – a Mandarin collar meets Mexican doll. Big boobs lose all definition hidden under a high neckline. It looks like someone has stuffed a bolster down Salma's front. And the balloon sleeves are overwhelming on her small frame.

Charlotte Church

✓ A deep, wide V neckline, tightly bound waist with a big loop attracting attention to the middle, long sleeves, a subtle, stylish print and sexy texture – this dress has got the lot, and Charlotte looks a million dollars.

✗ This outfit shows how difficult it is for an Hourglass to do casual. A big, bright, billowing top makes Charlotte look wide and boxy by obscuring her little waist, and jeans with flip flops shorten her legs.

The Cornet

'My body is like a boy's.
I find it difficult to look feminine'

Broad shoulders

Small boobs

No waist

Slim hips

Long, slim legs

The Cornet
YOUR SHAPE

IT'S QUITE POSSIBLE that as a young girl you were a tomboy, climbing trees and sharing your brother's clothes. This was great! Being one of the boys was the way you felt happiest. Your days back then were all about laddish games and larking around. You weren't meant to have a feminine bend to your body at thirteen.

Later, when those curves, along with your boobs, failed to sprout as you entered womanhood, resembling a boy became less appealing. You no longer wanted to be integrated into the boys' gang, you wanted to attract them instead.

With your triangular shape, you probably felt less sexy than your curvy companions who were experimenting with push-up bras and hip wiggling. Wearing saucy clothes was pointless without a decent D cup or waist to cinch in. So now you stick to vests, jeans and t-shirts… sporty gear that suits your athletic frame. You've tried the other stuff, more skirts and dresses, but they just seem to hang off you.

Take heart, dear Cornet… because it is this very same athletic build that is so perfect for the catwalk. All those fashion designers adore your boy/girl shape. They quite rightly reckon that on you their clothes move in a way that shows them to their best advantage. To couture queens, you are literally a human coat hanger.

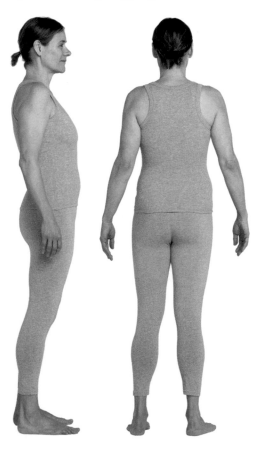

'IT IS THIS VERY SAME ATHLETIC BUILD THAT IS SO PERFECT FOR THE CATWALK'

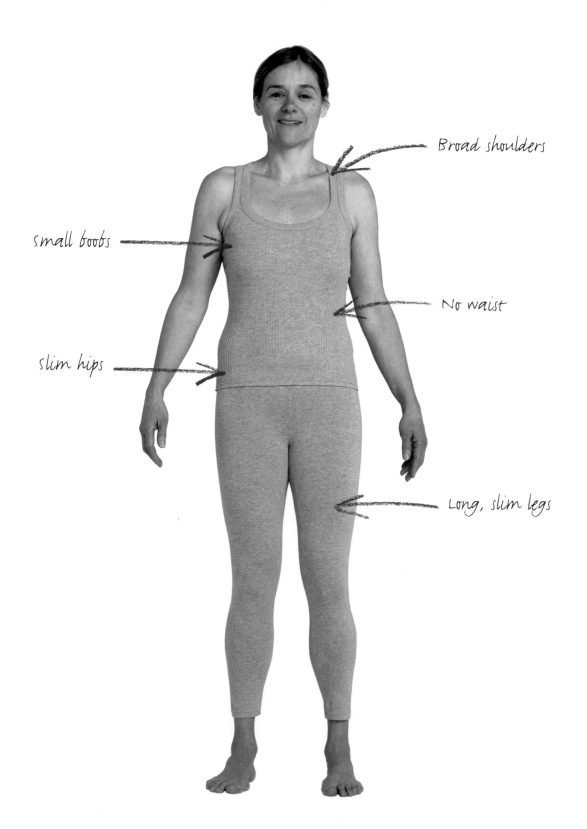

Broad shoulders

small boobs

No waist

slim hips

Long, slim legs

The Cornet
YOUR BIGGEST MISTAKES

REMEMBER ALICE – when she fell into Wonderland and drank that magic potion and, the next thing she knew, she grew so tall that her foot popped out the chimney and her arm smashed through the parlour window? Well, that's a bit what you look like in this get-up – a twelve-year-old schoolgirl with no breasts, bum or waist who has been run over by a steamroller.

Whenever these down-home, apple-pie looks come back on the merry-go-round of fashion, grab your apron and head for the hills. They are completely wrong for you.

You are an extreme shape and trying to disguise that will only make you look gawky and gangly. Learn instead to play up the drama of your angular body in everything you wear. Imagine yourself prancing down the catwalk of your life, pausing only to strike a great pose on each street corner.

Never wear

Shapeless floaty dresses
Platform shoes
Three-quarter sleeves
Scooped necklines
Cut-away shoulders
Shoulder pads

'TRYING TO DISGUISE YOUR SHAPE WILL ONLY MAKE YOU LOOK GAWKY AND GANGLY. LEARN INSTEAD TO PLAY UP THE DRAMA OF YOUR ANGULAR BODY IN EVERYTHING YOU WEAR'

The Cornet
KEY SHAPES

Cardigan

This cardigan works by creating dramatic angles to redraw the shape of your body. Broaden the collar to balance your shoulders then wrap the waist tightly to define your middle.

Angular dress

As with the cardigan, this dress helps to create dramatic shapes. The V shoulders dive inwards to a wide band emphasising your waist. The pockets jut out to exaggerate the width of your hips. Pinstripes reinforce the way this dress keeps the eye moving around your body.

Shirt

The wide lapels on this shirt break up the expanse of your shoulders and help bring the body back into proportion. The long double cuff can be worn unfolded to give added sleeve length.

Draping dress

This dress creates curves in all the right places. Draping jersey accentuates your limited shape. Clever use of off-centre gathers and diagonal lines will also help to create curves.

Jeans

The Cornet is one of the few shapes who looks fab in skinny jeans. They play up the slinkiness of your snake-like hips.

Fluted skirt

Your daytime skirt is a fluted shape to go in under the bottom, grasping it tightly and thus giving more shape to your hips.

Cigarette pants

Not many women can wear these 1950s inspired trousers, but they are great for you. The straight leg echoes and flatters your slim Cornet shape and then ends at a point to show off an elegant ankle. This re-proportions your body by breaking up the leg. Only someone with legs as long as the Cornet can get away with ankle length trousers.

Flared skirt

This net skirt is one of the best shapes for the Cornet. It flares straight out from the waist, so giving you shape. At the same time the net is stiff enough to hide any hint of a belly.

Shoes

With such slim calves and exquisite ankles, you need shoes that work a fine balance by using a delicate heel to its best advantage without overwhelming your legs.

Coat

Wide lapels halve your shoulder and the narrow horizontal stripes help to bring emphasis to your waist. A single button keeps the focus there. Big pockets help to build up your hips and add flounce.

Asymmetric wrap
cardigan

Angular dress

Wide lapel, fitted
shirt with double cuff

Asymmetric draping jersey dress

Skinny jeans

Fluted skirt

Cigarette pants

Flared skirt

Slim-heeled shoes

Single button coat with full skirt
and big hip pockets

The Cornet
YOUR BEST LOOK
CASUAL

YOU ARE AN angular kind of girl and your secret to looking stylish is to play up all those angles but not in an ironing board sort of a way. Rather, it is important for you to seek clothes that have lots of interestingly tailored seams, panels, long bits and short bits that wrap around and stick out to make your body into a work of art. Think Vivienne Westwood, think Issey Miyake, think Yohoji Yamamoto.

Here, the narrow stripes on this top create lots of great angles as the long ends of the cardigan criss-cross and wrap your body. Always be aware of sleeve length. Your arms, along with your legs, are likely to be long in proportion to your body. Wearing cuffs that stop an inch above your wrist will give you a gorilla-like demeanour. This top has luxuriously long sleeves so it looks like it was born to be worn by you. The wide diamond-shaped neckline is great for reducing the broadness of your shoulders. If you have lots of V-neck jumpers and t-shirts, a simple trick is to pull back the sides of the V with a couple of brooches or dress clips.

A flared skirt is a must-have in your wardrobe. The jutting line makes your waist look smaller and balances the width of your shoulders. Net skirts are particularly good for this, but for a daytime look we suggest a more tailored wool skirt.

Your slim, shapely legs need a slim, shapely heel. Chunky platforms would overwhelm those thoroughbred pins.

'THE NARROW
STRIPES ON
THIS TOP
CREATE LOTS
OF GREAT
ANGLES AS
THE LONG
ENDS OF THE
CARDIGAN
CRISS-CROSS
AND WRAP
YOUR BODY'

The Cornet
YOUR BEST LOOK
SMART

MOST PEOPLE NEED a smart jacket for smart occasions. For you that's an issue. So many jackets don't fit you properly. Either they're too tight across the back and shoulders, or they fit your shoulder and then swing freely around your middle. Then there's the eternal problem of the sleeves being too short.

Far better to invest in a couple of well-cut coats, one for the summer and one for winter. A coat that is fitted at your waist and then full-skirted gives you all the shaping you need. Flap pockets that stick out at the hip add an extra suggestion of curviness. Make sure that the coat fits you well at the shoulder. If necessary, have it taken in down the back seam so that it nestles lovingly into the scoop of your back.

Your legs are definitely your best assets so make sure they're always displayed to greatest advantage. Nothing looks sexier on a pair of shapely calves than fishnet tights and shapely heeled shoes.

'A COAT THAT IS FITTED AT YOUR WAIST AND THEN FULL-SKIRTED GIVES YOU ALL THE SHAPING YOU NEED'

'INVEST IN A COUPLE OF WELL-CUT COATS, ONE FOR THE SUMMER AND ONE FOR WINTER'

The Cornet
YOUR BEST LOOK
PARTY

WITH YOUR CLOTHES-HORSE figure you could carry off a bin liner with a couple of sequins scattered over it and still look good, but for evening we feel that you need to soften your look. Though not with frills and bows that your curvier sisters might wear. On you those would look just silly.

A column of chiffon lends fluidity and femininity to your shape while still retaining the sense of drama that a Cornet always needs. Clever folding and draping at the bust gives a more curvaceous aspect to your breasts and the wide-strapped halter neck helps to narrow the expanse of your shoulders.

High-heeled sandals with a shapely heel add an elegant finish to this flattering evening dress.

'CHIFFON LENDS FLUIDITY AND FEMININITY TO YOUR SHAPE WHILE STILL RETAINING THE SENSE OF DRAMA A CORNET NEEDS'

WHAT IT MEANS
TO BE A CORNET

* You are probably fed up to the teeth with people casting sideways glances and murmuring 'anorexic' into the back of their hands. You are naturally slim and there's nothing wrong with that. Next time you catch a disapproving look feel free to order yourself an extra scoop of icecream and then scoff the lot in front of your accuser – just to show them that you can.

* Every time spring and autumn come around you feel awkward because you have difficulty with long sleeves. No doubt you've heard endless sales assistants advising you that sleeves look really cool pushed up to three-quarter length. Don't do it. They are just trying to sell you something that doesn't fit. Three-quarter sleeves will make you look like a gorilla. Always check that there is enough hem in the sleeve to have it lengthened – at least two inches.

* Jacket and coat sleeves that are finished with a buttoned vent usually have a diagonal seam at the corner (this is called a mitred seam). These cannot be lengthened.

* A huge watch works nicely to fill in the gap between cuff and hand.

* In winter, invest in lots of long gloves for smart wear and wrist warmers for casual clothes. As well as giving a good finish to your arms, they keep the wind from blowing up your sleeves.

* As you get older you can develop a tummy. Start as early as possible doing exercise to improve your core strength – Pilates is ideal for this.

* Wear a low-leg swimsuit to make your body seem longer – you don't need to extend your legs.

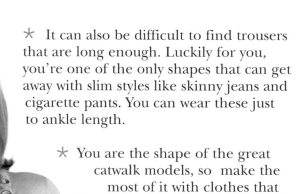

★ It can also be difficult to find trousers that are long enough. Luckily for you, you're one of the only shapes that can get away with slim styles like skinny jeans and cigarette pants. You can wear these just to ankle length.

★ You are the shape of the great catwalk models, so make the most of it with clothes that fold and drape around your body.

'YOU ARE THE SHAPE OF GREAT CATWALK MODELS, SO MAKE THE MOST OF IT WITH CLOTHES THAT FOLD AND DRAPE AROUND YOUR BODY'

CORNETS TO INSPIRE YOU...

Elle MacPherson

✓ Long-necked Cornets like Elle MacPherson can wear big collars with graceful elegance. The wide lapels on this jacket break up Elle's shoulder line while the little belt emphasises her waist. Fitted jeans are the best thing for showing off endless Cornet legs.

✗ Spaghetti straps will give any Cornet the shoulders of an Olympic swimmer and, even though she's gorgeous, Elle is no exception to the rule. The top of this dress drags down her boobs and makes them look saggy.

Cameron Diaz

✓ The Cornet is the only shape that can truly look amazing in skinny jeans. Here Cameron Diaz shows how to wear boys' clothes with panache. Spray on the jeans so that they show every bit of your sinuous legs. Don't worry that they stop at your ankles – you've got inches to spare. Wear a short jacket that breaks up your length and also cuts into the white t-shirt, giving the suggestion of a waist.

✗ This straight-up-and-down dress makes Cameron Diaz look like a black ironing board – with huge shoulders.

Naomi Campbell

✓ Broad straps are great for managing the size of a Cornet's shoulders. This dress sculpts Naomi Campbell's upper half giving her a slim waist. That effect is further enhanced by a silver band cutting under her bum and creating a curvy S shape. More silver bands help to break up the length of Naomi's legs.

✗ The cut-away shoulders and vertical design on this straight sheath dress lend a distinctly plank-like impression to Naomi's body.

The
Cello

'Whatever I wear, I always feel big'

Big boobs

Short waist

Big hips

Big bottom

Big thighs

Slim lower legs

The Cello
YOUR SHAPE

YOUR SHOULDERS ARE broad, your boobs are big, and your buttocks and thighs are in a class of their own. Yet you are all woman – a refined, beautifully tuned Cello.

It may be that on occasion you feel conspicuous compared to your more petite or slender friends. That's okay, you are! There's simply no point in trying to shrink away and hide. Once you've taken that on board and figured out how to just be you in fabulous, full-on outfits you will always turn every head as you sweep down the staircase or sashay onto the dance floor. You will never be one for wispy tops over tight jeans, and Hallelujah for that.

You are never the smallest instrument in Aphrodite's orchestra, but you certainly might be the proudest. Luckily, you have the bone structure to carry off those well-endowed features with grace and ease.

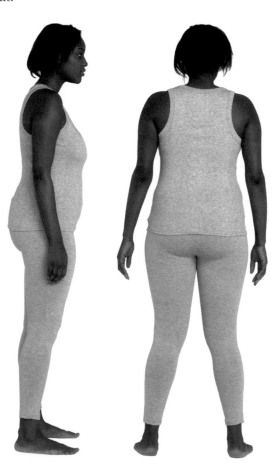

In times past you may have considered yourself a Pear. The truth is, you are nothing like her. Yes, your thighs are heavier, but your shape is balanced by broad shoulders and big tits. Your short waist is another defining feature.

As a Cello, the main thing you need to learn from us is how to stand tall and strut your stuff.

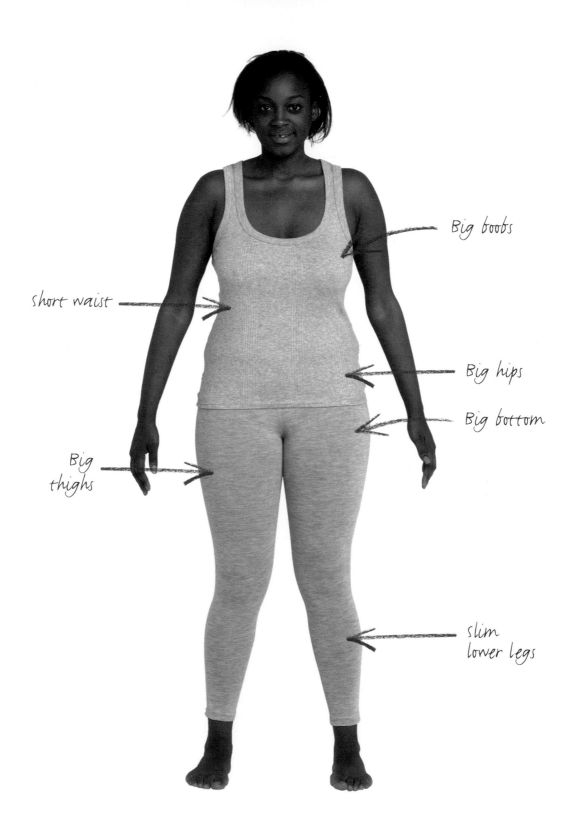

Big boobs

short waist

Big hips

Big bottom

Big thighs

slim
lower legs

The Cello
YOUR BIGGEST MISTAKES

OH, DARLING, why do you do this to yourself? Look at the size of those thighs and that bum in skinny white jeans. Yes, you do have fabulous calves and ankles and here they do look slim, but only in comparison to your upper leg.

Keep light, bright colours well away from that particular area. Likewise, avoid shiny fabrics. Satin or leather trousers will only turn your thighs into a couple of rubber inner tubes.

Meanwhile, you don't need to totally encase your upper half in a black polo-neck jumper in the hope that it will disappear altogether. It actually increases the size of your chest area and it's barely covering your midriff. One false move and the belly roll that has been squeezed up by those too-tight jeans will pop out like a jack-in-the-box.

Never wear

Pencil skirts
Mini skirts
Leather or satin trousers
Tight jeans
Ankle boots

'A BLACK POLO-NECK JUMPER ONLY INCREASES THE SIZE OF YOUR CHEST AREA...'

The Cello
KEY SHAPES

Top

A wide V neckline is more flattering than a narrow V on your broad shoulders. It works wonders to reduce your chest and shoulders and gives the best shape to your boobs.

Shirt

Make sure that your shirt is shaped into your waist and that the lapels don't fight with any jacket or coat you wear over it. Your outfits should have only one set of lapels at the top. This keeps your neckline open and free of clutter.

Dress

The wide halterneck shape will lift your boobs. A wide cummerbund lengthens your waist. The print on this dress sculpts your body with its variations of light and dark.

Coat

The A line of this coat covers your bum and slices your thighs in half. The flared sleeves give elegance to your waist and the wide lapel acts as a frame to your neck and décolleté.

Jumper

The open, round neckline shows off one of your best assets. Make sure that your jumper is long enough to cover and disguise your tummy with a few gentle folds.

Skirt

Sewn down panelling holds in your tummy at the front and cuts your bum in half at the back, while the pleats of the skirt allow flowing movement as you walk.

Jacket

Because you are short waisted it is important to wear jackets that elongate your body and give you a nipped-in waist. A very long lapel with a single button does both, as in this smoking jacket.

Trousers

As you have big haunches you must avoid side pockets at all times. Go for no-fuss trousers that are sufficiently wide legged to freely accommodate your thighs. Turn-ups will help to balance the width of your bum.

Earrings

A Cello is, by definition, of larger build. Your broad shoulders and proudly jutting breasts can tend to make your head seem smaller by comparison. A pair of fabulous rounded earrings will divert attention back to your face.

Shoes

Your legs are shapely and well defined below the knee, so go for a shoe that can support the size of your upper leg while still managing to make the most of your elegant ankles.

Wide V-neckline top

Shirt with no lapels

Wide-waisted dress
with halterneck

Flared coat with wide sleeves
and deep lapels

Scooped neck
jumper to hips

Panelled and pleated skirt

Long lapel, single
button jacket

No fuss, wide-legged trousers
with turn-ups

Fabulous earrings

Wedge with a platform

The Cello
YOUR BEST LOOK
CASUAL

HAVING BIG THIGHS makes wearing trousers a challenge for you. Jeans are pretty much out of the question. You need some well-cut, wide-leg trousers. No side pockets. Once you've found a pair that fit you around the upper leg, treasure them. Don't worry if they gape at the waist. It is a simple matter for a tailor to adjust that.

The other important consideration is that they must be long enough. Shortening your legs in any way will only encourage them to take on a barrel-like appearance. Your legs are proportionately long so you can get away with cuffs on trousers and they will help to balance the width of your bottom.

If you are lucky enough to know a good tailor or dressmaker, have a pattern made from those perfect trousers so that you can have a couple of new pairs every year.

Darker colours are most slimming on the legs. We always say that black looks great with black. The wide, deep lapels on this jacket cut into the breadth of your shoulders. A tuxedo jacket worn with a waistcoat might seem like party attire, but it is the lack of a shirt collar that gives it a casual air. You could equally wear this look with a white or dark blue t-shirt.

Leather shoes or boots with a chunky heel will give a balanced feel to your bottom half. In summer, try wearing this look with black tennis shoes or Converse trainers.

'HAVE A PATTERN MADE FROM THOSE PERFECT TROUSERS SO YOU CAN HAVE A COUPLE OF NEW PAIRS EVERY YEAR'

The Cello
YOUR BEST LOOK SMART

IT'S OKAY TO WEAR shiny fabric in this way. The shininess is diffused by a textured pattern that helps to break up your body, so we're not left with the impression of a woman encased in a metallic sausage skin. The key thing is that the coat is not sticking to, and thereby spotlighting, your thighs.

A more petite woman could not carry off such a bold coat as this, but you were born to wear it. The wide lapels break up your shoulder line while the flamboyant finishing of the sleeves draws our eyes out and away from your bottom end.

A V neckline showing just a flash of t-shirt beneath says: 'I'm all woman, but I'm still approachable.' Three central buttons make your waist seem longer.

Your lower legs are good, so don't throw the baby out with the bathwater by covering them up all the time. You need a pair of solid shoes to ground you and these chunky, curvy wedges do the job nicely.

'A MORE PETITE WOMAN COULD NOT CARRY OFF SUCH A BOLD COAT AS THIS...YOU WERE BORN TO WEAR IT'

The Cello
YOUR BEST LOOK
PARTY

IT'S TOUGH FOR YOU to find something to wear when going out clubbing. Skimpy tops and short, tight skirts are not your best friends. Yet you don't want to turn up at the night-time hot spot in a business suit or a full-on evening gown.

Here's a great solution. This dress is styled like a day dress, but is made in a silky fabric. Because it's long, it is definitely smarter than something you might wear to work, yet the all-over print gives it a more laid-back, less formal feel.

As far as body shaping qualities go, this dress is a winner all the way. The wide halter neck gives good support to your boobs while being low-cut enough to make sure that you're an eye catcher on the dance floor.

Halter necks are great for reducing broad shoulders. They may seem like a minor detail but your earrings are doing major work here. Look at how they draw attention to Julianna's face and at the same time make her head look bigger and more in proportion with her shoulders. The smallish print has the effect of giving more movement to the body, so making it seem curvier.

A deep, deep panelled band narrows and lengthens your short waist and the skirt is full enough to hide your thighs. You could wear this outfit with your black tuxedo jacket for full-on glamour or with a simple fitted white cardigan when you want to give off a more relaxed air.

'HALTER
NECKS ARE
GREAT FOR
REDUCING
BROAD
SHOULDERS'

WHAT IT MEANS
TO BE A CELLO

∗ You've never going to be a shrinking violet so make the most of it. Playing to your strengths will ensure that heads turn every time you walk into a room.

∗ You might love a mini skirt, but it's the most unflattering item in your wardrobe. When out clubbing, encase your thighs in leggings – they hold everything in place and allow you to get away with shorter skirt styles.

∗ At the beach, wear a sarong open down the front of one thigh. This will flatter the best part of your leg and deflect eyes away from your butt.

∗ Always wear your strongest, brightest colours up top.

∗ V necklines break up your top half. A wide V also lessens the breadth of your shoulders whereas a narrow V widens your shoulder line.

∗ If you want to stand out on the dance floor, try a metallic top.

★ You don't need a lot of jewellery. Use a pair of huge earrings for drama, otherwise use strong colours or patterns to attract attention to yourself.

★ For evening wear, don't bulk up your top half with layers of cardigan and jacket. Artfully drape a long wrap around your arms and chest.

'YOU ARE ONE OF THE MOST DESIRABLE WOMANLY SHAPES'

CELLOS
TO INSPIRE YOU...

Oprah Winfrey

✓ Sensational.
This is the perfect
dress for Oprah.
The wide V neckline
flatters her shoulders
and balances the size
of her bottom. Jersey
fabric lends a fluidity and
softness to her quite muscular
frame. A slightly flared over-
skirt is wide enough to
accommodate her bigger
thighs without straining,
but layered over a
slimmer underskirt it
gives the impression
of an elegant column.

✗ This jacket cuts Oprah
right across her widest part.
Shiny satin only highlights
how much her thighs are
straining to be free.

Kirstie Allie

✓ The shape of this neckline does such a great job of dividing Kirstie's bust into more manageable proportions. The big belt creates waist definition against a darker background. All the pattern is on the lower half of Kirtsie's skirt, drawing our eyes away from the width of her thighs.

✗ Pleating from the waist creates too much volume of fabric swirling around Kirstie's nether regions. The frilly, flouncy, rainbow-coloured cardigan is totally overwhelming and does nothing to give shape to her waist.

Serena Williams

✓ You think that having thunder thighs means concealing them under sackcloth forever? Wrong! Serena's split to the thigh gown has the effect of cutting a narrow slash through her leg, thereby skinnifying it. Backless shoes extend the line further, making her legs go on for days. The halter neck controls her boobs while the silver faux-belt reduces her waist to what looks like four inches. Game, set and match.

✗ The neckline of this top is too low and wide to enhance Serena's bust. She's just spilling out all over the place. Likewise, a skinny little belt is fighting a losing battle in trying to winch that sturdy waist, So far, so-so, but the real horror is yet to come... Thigh-sucking lycra pedal pushers make a mockery of any Cello, even one as fit as Serena. Don't let it happen to you.

The
Apple

'My tummy dictates how I dress'

Average tits

Tummy bigger than tits

Quite flat bum

OK legs

The Apple
YOUR SHAPE

THE APPLE, by definition, is round. Smooth and luscious, your form is as soft and cosy as the down on a peach. You have the body people want to cuddle up to. But is it easy to dress? No, it isn't. That's why you think it is so much safer to cover yourself with yards of fabric, making absolutely sure not one centimetre of flesh can peep out.

Sometimes the Apple shape materialises with the onset of menopause. As if hot flushes, wrinkles and crinkling skin weren't enough, Mother Nature took it upon herself to add to her list of horrors thickened waistlines that steal away any lasting feelings of being a woman. Sadly, it's a fact of female life, and one that we have to live with.

At the earlier end of the sliding scale is the plump young cub possessing a little puppy fat. This usually disappears with age, but whether it's there for the rest of your life or is a momentary hormonal upheaval, it probably makes you feel pretty rotten.

Out of all our shapes, the Apple tends to be the one with the least self-confidence. Irrespective of your beautiful skin, pillow-soft breasts and divinely sculpted ankles, you really don't like your body. It makes you want to hide away. But don't do it. Don't deprive others of your wonderful cleavage that can easily be enhanced with low tops and fitted jackets.

Your body is so easy to redefine with the right clothes.

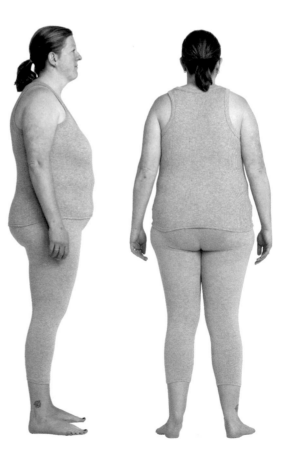

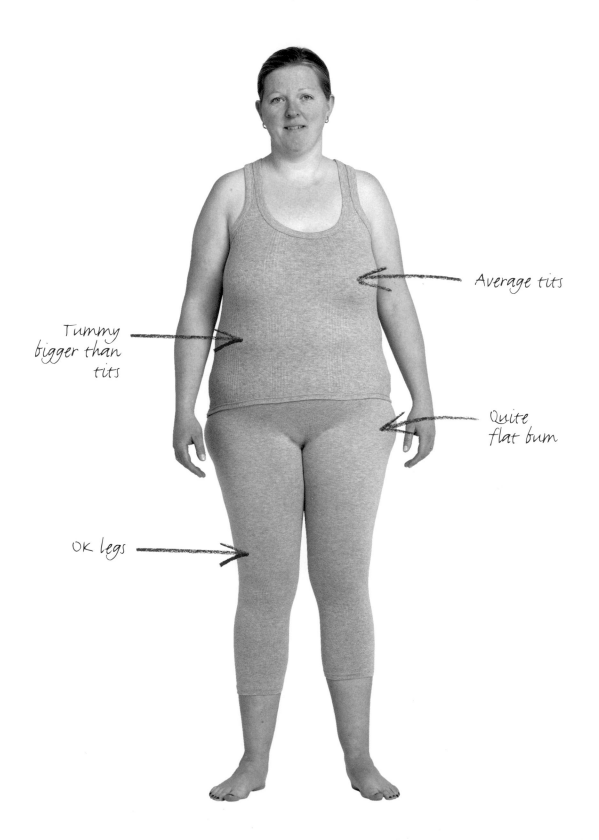

Average tits

Tummy bigger than tits

Quite flat bum

OK legs

The Apple
YOUR BIGGEST MISTAKES

SO, IS THIS HOW you have been doing it? Dressing like a builder, covering those lumps and bumps with as much fabric as you can. In doing this, you really are destroying any hope of making the most of your shape.

Take a look at these jeans – they are huge, they are masculine and the narrowness of the tapered legs serves only to maximise your top heaviness. You buy them big so that the high waistline will fit around your middle.

Then the jacket. Ugh! These shapeless, non-edifying garments in waterproof nylon or, God forbid, fleece, balloon you to vast proportions, as does the high neckline of your top. Then you think, 'Oh, I hate my hair too, so I'll just scrape it back to ensure that I erase any semblance of femininity whatsoever.'

The crux of what is going on is that you dislike your body, so you make the big mistake of covering it up and in doing so you lose sight of yourself completely. It's a crime worthy of exile to a far distant planet. Draping yourself in nondescript clobber will not make you disappear, rather it will make you into a highly visible but shapeless blob.

Far better to learn to love and be proud of your body – then show the world what you've got with every last ounce of flair and conviction.

Never wear
Tight t-shirts
Big square t-shirts
High-waisted trousers
Pleated waists
Puffa jackets
Men's jeans

'DRESSING LIKE THIS...YOU REALLY ARE DESTROYING ANY HOPE OF MAKING THE MOST OF YOUR SHAPE'

The Apple
KEY SHAPES

Top
This top encircles and highlights your body at the slimmest point, just under your boobs. It is loose enough to skim your tum, but doesn't flare outwards. Small sleeves cover your upper arms.

T-shirt
You absolutely must have a t-shirt that is ruched on the middle. The small gathers will confuse the eye into not knowing which bit is flab and which bit is fabric. Make sure the t-shirt is long enough to comfortably cover your tum. A wide V neckline breaks up the size of your chest and the softly draped sleeves won't cut into your arms.

Trousers
Your smartest trousers will be flat fronted with a deep waistband. They fasten on the side so as to avoid adding any extra bumps to your belly. The legs are wide and don't cling to your tum, bum or thighs at any point.

Shirt
Make sure that your shirt goes in under your boobs and either zips at the side or has a hook and eye corset closure down the front. This will give you wonderful shape and support at the same time. The wide detail at the cuff draws the eye down and thins out your arms. Make sure your shirts don't button all the way up to the top. Shirts with open fronts are more flattering for your shape.

Jacket
The usual denim jacket will make you look big and square up top, so choose one with more tailoring and an open V neck. A tie at the waist is great because the knot and trailing ends of the belt or sash help to hide the bulge of your tum.

Coat
A straight duster coat, worn open against a contrasting fabric, will break your body up into three long, slim slices. The small tone-on-tone pattern diverts the eye so that your coat doesn't look like one big block of colour. If you are a short Apple, be careful that the coat ends above your knee. If you are taller, you can afford to take it to just below the knee.

Skirt
Your skirt should always be side fastening and flat fronted. The inverted box pleats start at a point below your tum so they don't add any extra bulk.

Denim trousers
Traditional jeans just don't work for you. Look out instead for tailored, wide-legged trousers in denim or indigo cotton.

Low shoes
A small, shaped wedge gives you stability yet shows off the slim shapeliness of your calves and ankles.

High shoes
And a higher version of the same shoes, for evening wear.

Tight, under the boobs, tummy-skimming top

Ruched on the middle t-shirt

Flat-fronted trousers

Side fastening long sleeved shirt

Tie waist jacket

Straight duster coat

Skirt with pleats starting below the tummy

Small shaped wedge

Tailored trousers in demin

Higher shaped wedge

The Apple
YOUR BEST LOOK
CASUAL

FOR YOU, IT'S ALL ABOUT bringing focus to the top half, up and away from your tummy. In the past you have been covering up your entire body because you were not confident about your boobs and belly.

Start by loving yourself enough to invest in a decent bra. Go and get properly measured and fitted. You may be surprised to find that you are not the size you thought you were. The straps will need constant hoiking up and should be checked each time you get dressed to make sure that they haven't got longer during the previous wear. A good bra can be pricey, but is worth every penny. Just look at the difference that decent upholstery has made to Sue's shape.

The top has a wide-open neckline that gives us a flash of the beginning of your cleavage. It's a sure-fire way to keep people's eyes away from your tum. If you do have a big tummy it is certain that your slimmest part will be just under your boobs. This top clings tightly and flatteringly at that point and then flares just enough to skim over the lumps below. The dark colour is slimming while a pattern breaks up your middle. Cap sleeves help to broaden your shoulders.

If you have big arms, you don't have to spend your entire life swaddled in batwing sleeves. Make sure that the very top of your arm is always covered and that the sleeves cup your upper arms, rather than squeeze them like a sausage skin. If necessary, have small darts let into your sleeves under the arm.

Look out for tailored trousers that have no bulky pockets or protruding zippers. Side-fastening trousers are ideal. The waistband should be low and wide enough to sit flatly on your tum. Too high and it will squeeze you out the top like a toothpaste tube – too low and excess folds will hang over. These trousers are slightly flared at the bottom so they give a good balance to your belly.

Avoid clumpy shoes – they will make your legs seem heavier than they really are. Your whole body shape sits well atop a dainty wedge.

'A WIDE-OPEN NECKLINE IS A SURE-FIRE WAY TO KEEP PEOPLE'S EYES AWAY FROM YOUR TUM'

The Apple
YOUR BEST LOOK SMART

IT IS POSSIBLE TO WEAR lighter shades when you are larger, as with this outfit. The combination of a flat grey with the texture of the cream broderie-anglaise coat breaks up your frame and gives your curves more emphasis. Note that the darker shade of grey is still on your bottom half and that the trousers conform to the 'wide leg, side-fastening' rule.

A long coat worn open is a really valuable way for you to look smart and slimmer at the same time. The vertical lines created by the front opening of the coat seemingly dissect your body into three long, narrow slices. Not all Apples are as tall as Sue, so remember to have your coat altered to keep it in proportion with your body so that it doesn't swamp you. Make sure, also, that your coat contrasts against your outfit underneath. If everything is the same colour it will have the undesirable effect of making you seem bigger, not smaller. Because the coat is busy, a simple pendant will suffice to break up your middle section.

Sparkly sandals give a smart but laid-back finish.

'THE COMBINATION OF A FLAT GREY WITH THE TEXTURE OF THE CREAM BRODERIE-ANGLAISE COAT BREAKS UP YOUR FRAME AND GIVES YOUR CURVES MORE EMPHASIS'

The Apple
YOUR BEST LOOK PARTY

IT'S AMAZING HOW MUCH body sculpting can be achieved with clever use of colour, pattern and texture. To make the most of your Apple shape it's really important to learn how those principles work.

Wearing all one colour or a dress in an all-over big print will seemingly add two sizes to your appearance. Combining plain and print, or plain and texture, breaks up and re-shapes your silhouette.

Here a busy pattern in the middle does a great job of disguising the size of your tum. The short cardigan further breaks up your body, while its loose sleeves veil your upper arms.

The skirt hangs straight so that it doesn't widen you, but the box pleats give it fluidity. We cannot stress how important it is that the inverted pleats start below your tummy. In this way you create a flat line leading our eyes downwards. From the side the skirt does not cup under your belly but travels straight down concealing the bulk of your tummy.

For evening, these shoes are higher than your first pair but the principle is the same – a shaped wedge that supports you and shows off the slim shapeliness of your calves and ankles.

'COMBINING
PLAIN AND
PRINT, OR
PLAIN AND
TEXTURE,
BREAKS UP
AND RE-SHAPES
YOUR
SILHOUETTE…
DISGUISING
THE SIZE OF
YOUR TUM'

WHAT IT MEANS TO BE AN APPLE

∗ To get to love the shape that you are, try lying in your bed naked for an hour. Once you've accepted that, go to bed and sleep naked all night long. Enhance the experience with a set of new Egyptian cotton sheets.

∗ We always say, start with the underwear, and especially the bra. With you, this is the most important thing to get right before you hit the shops to try on these exciting new shapes we have chosen for you. It will make you feel more confident about your shape.

∗ Remember that you are probably a size or two smaller on your shoulders than your tummy, so if you buy to fit your tummy your jackets and coats will just look huge on you. Always buy the jacket to fit your shoulders and not your middle. Use a scarf to fill the gap and warm your front.

∗ If you suffer from water retention, as many Apples do, don't shop on those days. You will always buy the wrong clothes.

∗ On the beach, you can break some rules. Take pleasure in finding the loudest, funkiest colours and wild printed kaftans, then wear them with pride.

∗ Your biggest asset is your cleavage. LEARN to love your boobs. First, buy a luxurious bust cream. Next, spend 10% of your clothing budget on bras. The lift they give will flatten your tummy and streamline your silhouette.

∗ Experiment with colour, pattern and texture – getting this right will have a really positive impact on how you dress.

'YOUR
BIGGEST
ASSET IS
YOUR
CLEAVAGE.
LEARN TO
LOVE YOUR
BOOBS'

* The puffa is your nemesis.
Invest in thermal underwear and
a raincoat that has shape instead.
Don't let a casual situation make
you lazy in your dress.

APPLES
TO INSPIRE YOU...

Jo Brand

✔ We have to confess, we did this one ourselves. Jo Brand is a classic Apple and, like many of her sisters in shape, she had tended to go in for the big-baggy-bordering-on-menswear style of dressing. A long, straight skirt falling all the way to the floor gives a column-like outline to her silhouette. Wearing a long coat in a darker shade creates two vertical lines that, in effect, slice her body into three long thin strips. Jo's top is the right length to extend her legs, but not so short as to cut across her tum. A bit of jewellery never did a girl any harm either.

✘ At first glance you might think that this outfit is similar to Jo's good look, but on closer inspection it becomes apparent that the principles are very different. Firstly, all-over black washes the colour from Jo's skin. The longer line top makes her upper half appear huge and, conversely, her legs pint-sized. Tapering trousers lend a teetering 'Humpty-Dumpty' feel to her look. Lastly, Jo's coat, while it is long, is also black so it blends with her body to make it seem bigger. Leather is too bulky and shapeless for an Apple; better to choose more flowing fabrics. We won't even discuss the shoes.

Kathy Bates

✓ Whoever said that an Apple can't look drop dead gorgeous? The bodice of this gown is cut to lift Kathy Bates' boobs whilst holding in her tummy. Ruching and pleating across the entire top half will disguise any bumps that might stray out. The diaphanous jacket veils her arms without detracting one little bit from the glamour of the look.

✗ What not to do if you're an Apple: shorten your legs with ankle-skimming trousers, making sure that they are also tapered to exaggerate the size of your top half. Next, draw all eyes to your middle by wearing a light coloured top and cardigan and then cut your silhouette in half by creating maximum contrast between the colours on your upper and lower body.

Beth Ditto

✓ We just adore the way that Beth Ditto makes a virtue of her Apple shape. There's no body shame with this lady. The wide neckline opens her chest and lifts her boobs. A big silver waistband breaks up her middle section. The whole outfit clearly shows that you don't need to hide yourself away, you can look glamorous and fabulous with the best of them.

✗ Aaargh. We're all in favour of flaunting what you've got, but not in all over tartan from neck to knee. On Beth, this check dress looks like some sort of bizarre measuring graph.

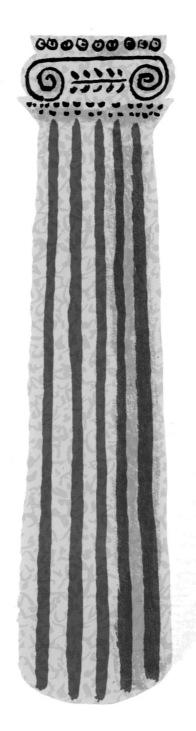

The
Column

'With my shape, I always play it safe'

Shoulder width
same as hip width

Slight waist

Longer legs

The Column
YOUR SHAPE

`TAKE A LOOK at your old school photograph (if you have kept it). Found yourself… the girl a head taller than the rest? Mmmm. We bet you suffered from growing pains as you shot up faster than your classmates.

You have always found it difficult to find clothes to fit: to get enough length in the sleeve of a jacket or a trouser leg you have had to compromise on overall fit. Consequently your style might have teetered on the edge of scarecrow chic. Your wardrobe might be a bit of a shambles, in spite of your friends thinking you have rather a good form for fashion. Being mostly tall, Columns can carry clothes well. It's just a question of knowing which shops to head for as much as which styles to choose.

The really difficult time for you ladies is menopause. The figure that looked magically put together, can become an alien being. Once your tummy stops listening to diets and exercise, your long limbs start to become difficult to accommodate. Body change can affect your whole attitude to clothes. You lose sight of what colours suit you and disregard the fact that your statuesque build continues to be fabulous.

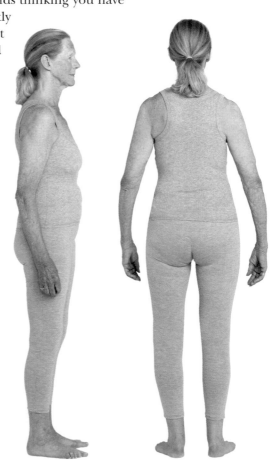

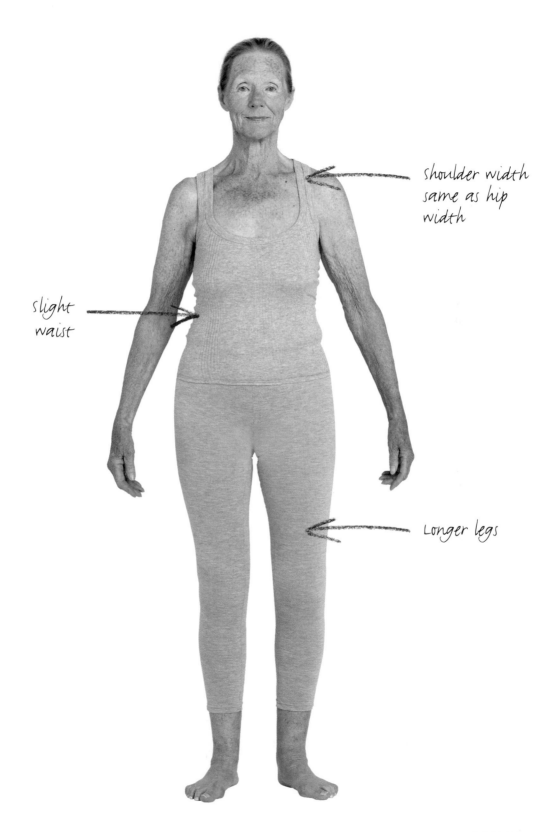

shoulder width
same as hip
width

slight
waist

Longer legs

The Column
YOUR BIGGEST MISTAKES

OH, COLUMN, we didn't mean you to take us at our word and dress yourself up as a pillar of salt. Wearing drab and shapeless clothes is not a good idea for any body shape, but on you it's a double shame because, with your perfect proportions, it only takes the slightest attention to style for you to look fabulous. Yet here you are, frumping about the place on the grounds of 'comfort'. Well, what's more comfortable about dull dishcloth blue than, say, passionate purple with a slash of aubergine?

You need strong blocks of colour to help define your body, and the same goes for cut. Straight up and down clothes do your figure no favours. You will always look better in a dramatic dress with a giant sash or a kimono top over flared trousers – garments we could imagine Marlene Dietrich swanning around in. Avoid anything ill-defined or, as in this case, completely pointless.

Never wear

Formless three-quarter
  length jackets
Straight dresses
Dropped waists
Cropped tops

'WEARING DRAB AND SHAPELESS CLOTHES IS NOT A GOOD IDEA FOR ANY SHAPE, BUT ON YOU IT'S A DOUBLE SHAME'

The Column
KEY SHAPES

Jumper

The classic round-neck jumper gives a very elegant shape to your body. Wear it with either long or short sleeves.

Jacket

Angular shapes are great on you. The idea is for everything to point to your middle. Flared sleeves, pointed hemline and a single button fastening all do exactly that.

Dress

Feminine chiffon softens your shape. The fluted long sleeves add volume at your extremities.

Coat

A three-quarter-length coat is great for showing off your legs and always looks youthful, whether you're seventeen or seventy. It's important that your coat is belted. Wear it tied at the back or tightly wrenched around your middle. Hip pockets add a bit of curve.

Skirt

The gentle flare of a true A-line is all you need to add a little shapeliness to your waist.

Cropped trousers

There's no need for you to fear the cropped trouser as a short-legged person should. It is a great way to break up the Column and show off your long legs. In winter, wear with flat leather boots. And in summer, wear wedges or flip flops.

Shirt

Gathering and pleating create separate and distinct areas defined by their texture. The upper pleated panel, the tucked waist and the two-part sleeve all help to break up the endlessness of the Column.

Trousers

You can wear almost any shape trouser, but this is a great staple to have in your wardrobe. The slight flare gives a hint of shapeliness. This will work with all of your tops.

Necklace

Long, chunky necklaces should be a staple in your wardrobe. They focus attention on the centre of your body and add drama to every outfit.

Shoes

The heel should be not too thin, not too thick, just a lovely balance and supportive. You don't need shoes that are too curvy.

Round-neck jumper

Angular, single button jacket

Chiffon dress with fluted long sleeves

A-line Skirt

Belted three-quarter-length coat with hip pockets

Shaped and gathered shirt

Slightly flared trousers

Cropped trousers

Long, chunky necklace

Elegantly balanced shoes

The Column
YOUR BEST LOOK
CASUAL

YOU HAVE LOVELY long legs, lithe arms and not too much flab around your girth... your only downfall is your need for shape. Your silhouette is cylindrical.

The most useful way to counter that is to break up your body. Wearing a plain, straight dress in a plain, flat colour is not a good plan. You need differentiation created by the use of colour, and tricks to draw the eye in all directions. What works very well on you are shapes that flare out at your extremities – bell bottom trousers and fluted sleeves. These help to draw your middle inwards.

The proportions of this outfit work very well because the trousers show off your long legs. To create shape, we still need to see your narrow thigh. With trousers this flared, never wear a coat longer than three-quarters otherwise it will cover up all the good work that your trousers are doing. Wearing the coat open breaks up the top beneath and tying the belt behind gives a great outline.

What makes this outfit really flow is the use of colour. Anne's bottom half is a tiny bit bigger than her top, so the darkest shade of green is in the trousers and the lightest shade in her top. That lifts the mid tone of the coat. This is sculpting by colour.

A big necklace is a key item for your Column shape. It will draw the emphasis away from your straight up and down outline and into the centre of your body. Ideally it should end somewhere between just below your boobs and your tummy button. Inspired use of colour will make necklaces the lynch pins that tie all your outfits together and make even the simplest jeans and t-shirt look smart and eye catching. Start collecting now.

The Column
YOUR BEST LOOK SMART

THE SECRET TO the success of this outfit is that everything works together to draw a high, neat waist. Your long, bold necklace acts as an arrow directing our eyes to the line that has been created by the high waist of your skirt. A single button jacket will always concentrate eyes on the centre of your torso. A long A-line skirt pushes your waist upwards giving you a more womanly shape.

The kitten heels add delicacy and curve to your straight figure. Tight, fitted boots create a good contrast between the flare of skirt and the narrowness of your leg.

'HERE EVERYTHING WORKS TOGETHER TO DRAW A HIGH, NEAT WAIST... GIVING YOU A MORE WOMANLY SHAPE'

The Column
YOUR BEST LOOK
PARTY

THIS OUTFIT LOOKS fabulous because it follows all the principles for your Column shape. The big tie sash allows you to position your waist precisely and put a focus firmly in the centre of your body. After you have followed our pointers for a while you will just feel naked without a necklace. It completes all your outfits. With this particular necklace, the descending gold discs act as another arrow to your waist.

Strong blocks of colour are a dramatic way for you to break up your cylindrical shape. Don't be afraid of a bold pattern either. It will always look more at home on your frame than a dainty print.

The wide hem of the trousers echoes the shape of the kimono sleeves, again adding volume at your extremities. With this outfit, everything yet again points towards your middle, like the ribbon on a beautifully wrapped gift.

'AFTER YOU HAVE FOLLOWED OUR POINTERS FOR A WHILE YOU WILL JUST FEEL NAKED WITHOUT A NECKLACE. IT COMPLETES ALL YOUR OUTFITS'

WHAT IT MEANS TO BE A COLUMN

✱ Columns can go in for tomboy looks. You are the one woman who can get away with wearing your husband's shirts and jackets. Make sure they fit your frame and always add a drop dead feminine touch. Think Katharine Hepburn rather than Kathy Bates.

✱ Your arms are long so you have a really hard time finding shirts. Look for shirts with double cuffs, then wear them unfolded for extra length.

✱ Sadly, most high street stores skimp on fabric. Zara is a great shop for long trousers with generous hems that can be let down even further.

✱ Bell sleeves give a shapely elegance to your arms. Practise being expressive and expansive while wearing them.

✱ If you have loads of too-short trousers, take them up and wear them as Capri pants (three-quarter length) or Plus Fours (knee length).

✱ Three-quarter sleeves, on the other hand, are neither here nor there on you, so have them taken up to the elbow.

✱ You are perfectly proportioned, so you don't need to play down any part. Strong blocks of colour can be worn everywhere. Make the most of it and have fun.

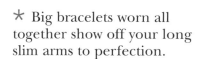 Big bracelets worn all together show off your long slim arms to perfection.

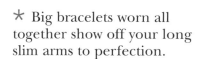 Keep your accessories big and bold. They should be the signature to your outfit, rather than a footnote. Avoid dinky little bags on a long strap, and stay away from fiddly necklaces and bangles.

'STRONG COLOUR CAN BE WORN EVERYWHERE. MAKE THE MOST OF IT AND HAVE FUN'

COLUMNS
TO INSPIRE YOU...

Gwyneth
Paltrow

✓ Like all great dresses
for Columns, this one
gives curves to a straight
body. The way the fabric
fans over the boobs and
around the lower leg
creates Hourglass
proportions. Ten out
of ten for Gwyneth.

✗ With a near perfectly
proportioned body,
Gwyneth Paltrow has to
work really hard to look
bad in clothes... so we
guess she must have been
up all night putting this
outfit together. It lacks
shape, it lacks colour,
it is a festival of frump.

Jane Fonda

✓ Jane Fonda can be a real tomboy, but equally can turn on the femininity full blast. This is the ultimate dress for a Column. Flaring at the extremities, it exaggerates the smallness of her tightly wrapped waist. Chiffon adds a feminine touch to a boyish figure. The layered skirt creates swishy movement around an angular silhouette.

✗ This washboard-style pinny flattens Jane's figure to the extent that if she turned sideways she would disappear.

Nicole Kidman

✓ This dress makes great use of a dramatic angle to break up Nicole Kidman's Column shape. The shiny, clingy fabric accentuates her waist and all the curves she does have.

✗ A high collar and dropped waist conspire together to turn Nicole's form into a long, shapeless, black cylinder.

The
Bell

*'My bum is wider than my shoulders.
I can never find a dress to fit me'*

Small shoulders

Small tits

Small waist

Short waist

Big thighs

Big bottom

The Bell
YOUR SHAPE

IN YOUR TEENS and twenties you were a small lady with a nice round bottom. As the years have advanced so has your butt. What happens to you is the quintessential, hateful middle-age spread. Your lower half becomes disproportionately large. It's a bugbear, but it's also a fact of life for many petite women. To combat this reality you might well be tempted take on the I-don't-care-about-clothes attitude to hide your inner voice telling you that your clothes are decidedly old before their time. If you are not careful, you, quicker than most, will disappear into tapered trousers with elasticated waists as your life slides into old lady-dom way before your time. Any sexiness you purveyed will have declined with your wardrobe as you have no idea how to combat what you believe is a body not worth the bother.

Stop right there. You know that we will not countenance such a negative self-image; otherwise you wouldn't even bother to read this book. Your attitude is born out of despair, rather than genuine disdain for all things girly. You are still a petite, pretty woman who, with a little guidance, can dust off those skirts and dresses, that fun and froth, and quickly regain some femininity back into your life.

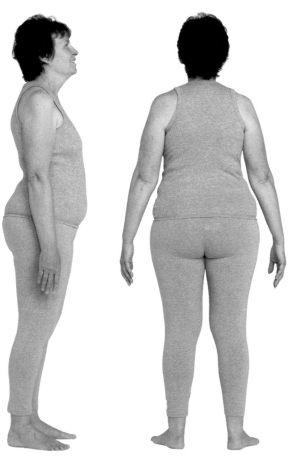

'THE MIDDLE-AGE SPREAD... IS A FACT OF LIFE FOR MANY PETITE WOMEN'

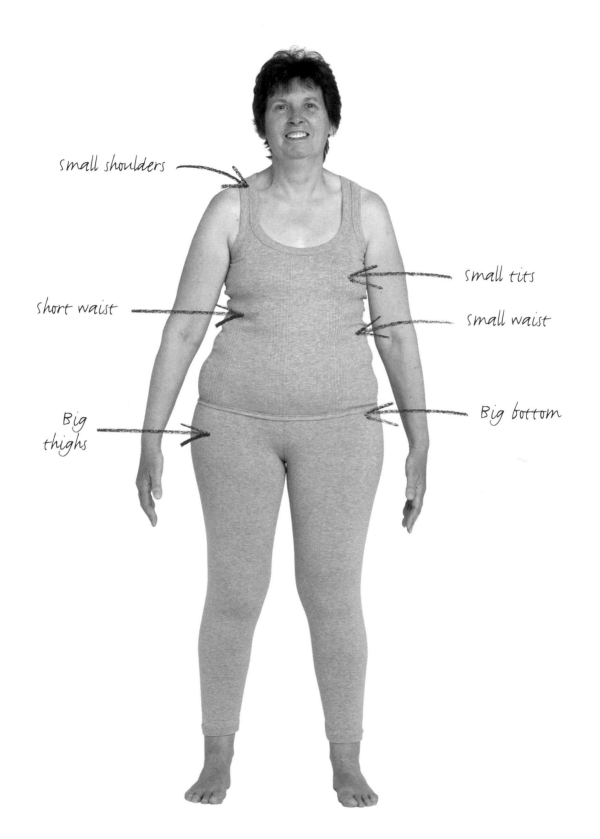

small shoulders

small tits

short waist

small waist

Big
thighs

Big bottom

The Bell
YOUR BIGGEST MISTAKES

THE MENTION of a summer wedding is enough to give you the cold sweats and shivers. Your dreams become haunted by images of frothy, floaty chiffon-clad damsels gliding across manicured lawns as effortlessly as a stand of flamingos, their tinkling laughter breaking icily above your head as you fossick through the undergrowth like a lost Heffalump... and all this because that cursed woman in the 'formal wear' department told you that 'this is the perfect thing for a smart occasion, madam'. Well, let's get one thing straight: cut-on-the-bias chiffon dresses are your biggest mistake. Teaming them with your old black shoes and a few beads to cheer up the look is indicative of the fact that you don't really want to engage with dressing at all.

You really must learn to trust your own judgement, but you've lost so much self-confidence that you don't know where to start. We promise that the looks that follow will always work for you. Once you have gained confidence with those, you can start to experiment and rebuild your style.

Never wear

Balloon sleeves

Tapered trousers

Skimpy vests

Tiny neck chains

Wide V necklines

Bias-cut dresses

Anything fussy on
   your bottom half

'CUT-ON-THE-BIAS CHIFFON DRESSES ARE YOUR BIGGEST MISTAKE'

The Bell
KEY SHAPES

Gilet
This is the key to your key shapes. This bulky gilet rebalances your top half with your bottom, without compromising your waist. Make sure that it ends at the top of your hips.

Coat
One key trick for re-proportioning your body is to create broader shoulders. A funnel-shaped coat will do this beautifully. The buttons high on the chest bring emphasis to your top half. The coat then goes to an A-line at the most flattering point.

Shirt
Keeping necklines cut close to your neck broadens your shoulders. The tiny ruffles give the added bulk you need on the top half of your body while the central panel defines a high neat waist.

Kaftan
Go for a thigh-skimming kaftan in the summer to cover a swimsuit-embarrassed body. As you have long legs in proportion to the rest of your body this will end at the most flattering place. Added sequin detail around the collar will bring eyes up to your top half again.

Jumper
Bulk, bulk, bulk up your top half. This cowl neckline creates a broader shoulder. Try twisting and pinning it with a big, eye-catching brooch.

Trousers
Always go for side-fastening, loose and flowing trousers so you won't feel that your tummy is bulging over the waistband or your bottom is too tightly restrained. Never, ever, go near a tapered trouser.

Dress
The narrow neckline and long sleeves extend the line of your shoulders. A wide belt shows off your neat waist without shortening it.

Skirt
The heavy fabric in this skirt will contain your bottom and just where the pressure begins to get too much, relief is introduced in the shape of a strategically inserted pleat, allowing freedom for your legs to move. The skirt could have one kick pleat or several – the important principle is that they start at the bottom of your bottom so don't add any extra fullness.

Necklace
An eye-catching necklace is your best friend. It will help to show off the neatness of your upper frame and bring all eyes to the centre of your body.

Shoes
A cone heel has thickness to balance out your bottom half, combined with delicacy to give a feminine touch by showing off your slim ankles. Keep your shoes very simple at the front, avoiding any ankle straps or t-bars.

Bulky gilet

Funnel coat

Ruffled shirt with narrow
neckline

Thigh-length kaftan

Cowl neck jumper

Flowing, side-fastening
trousers

A-line shirt dress

Kick pleat skirt

Elaborate
necklace

Cone heel shoes

The Bell
YOUR BEST LOOK
CASUAL

YOUR TOP HALF is tiny compared to your bottom half, so all of your outfits need to be working to restore harmony between the two.

Using texture to achieve balance is a great skill for you to learn and to keep in your armoury. The bulky gilet that Jenny is wearing is a vital piece of kit for you. It could be sheepskin, fake fur, chunky knit or quilted. The point is that it adds volume to your top half. It's important to understand that this garment must be sleeveless and worn over another, thinner top or dress. Anything with bulky sleeves will swamp your small frame and turn you into a pint-sized Michelin lady. It is always a good idea for you to pick a top that draws the eye upwards, so vibrant colours work well.

A necklace also helps to capture our gaze.

So, now you've added size, shape and colour to your top half, all that's left to do is minimise attention on your bottom portion. Your trousers should be wide legged and made in a softly draping jersey fabric. They should be long enough to reach all the way to the ground. They should always be a darker colour than your top. That's all there is to it.

'THE BULKY GILET IS A VITAL PIECE OF KIT FOR YOU... IT ADDS VOLUME TO YOUR TOP HALF'

The Bell
YOUR BEST LOOK SMART

WHILE THE GILET with trousers look will become your uniform for everyday wear, on some smart occasions you just don't feel dressed without a jacket. Wearing a jacket over a gilet would puff you up to absurd proportions.

So how do you achieve that balanced silhouette without your trusty best friend? You turn to your other best friend, the cowl neck jumper. It does a fabulous job of focusing attention on your top half.

Your jacket should be in a lighter colour than your trousers and it is essential that the hemline sits just above the top of your bum. Any longer and it will work against you by accentuating your widest part.

Your trousers will always follow the same principles, but remember that the trousers that you wear with heels must be longer than the trousers you wear with trainers.

'YOUR OTHER BEST FRIEND IS THE COWL NECK JUMPER... IT DOES A FABULOUS JOB OF FOCUSING ATTENTION ON YOUR TOP HALF'

The Bell
YOUR BEST LOOK
PARTY

WE THINK IT HAS BEEN established that chiffon, cut-on-the-bias, spaghetti-strap party dresses are not your thing. In fact, you have so much trouble finding dresses of any description to fit both on your top and bottom that it probably doesn't even occur to you to look on the dress rails any more. It really is time to re-evaluate that prejudice. Finding the one fabulous, right dress will change how you feel about yourself. Make sure it fits you flatteringly on top and that the skirt of the dress is full enough to flow around your nether regions without clinging as you walk.

This purple dress is near perfection. Its cap sleeves jut outwards, extending your shoulder line. The deep cummerbund makes your waist longer and that makes you appear taller.

You will always wrestle with finding new ways to emphasise your upper body. An elaborate necklace that completely fills your décolletage is a superb attention-grabber.

To walk with a feminine movement you need to wear dresses that create movement of fabric swishing around your thighs without adding any extra bulk to your haunches. The pleats on this dress start low on your hip. They are small and flat, creating vertical lines to draw our eyes downwards.

Never wear embroidery, lace or sequins on your bottom half.

Dainty shoes are perfect for your slim ankles, but a kitten heel would give your shape a precariously teetering feel. Although this cone heel is an unusual shape, it's worth hunting out because it is perfect for you.

'FINDING
THAT ONE
FABULOUS,
RIGHT
DRESS WILL
CHANGE
HOW YOU
FEEL ABOUT
YOURSELF'

WHAT IT MEANS TO BE A BELL

* If you are invited to a wedding, alarm bells ring. Dresses can be difficult, so if you can't find your dream dress, go for a suit. Search out shops that will sell two halves of a suit in different sizes. M&S, John Lewis and Principles are really helpful.

* Your short waist means that many tops are just too long for your shape. Find your tops in the petite department.

* Shops like Jigsaw and Kew are great for A-line skirts.

* Don't depress yourself by looking for the latest dresses every summer. The two styles in this book are the ones that suit you so keep an eye out for those and don't waste your time trying on the latest fads.

* Friends may have told you to always wear a long line jacket to cover your thighs. They are trying to be helpful, but it's best to ignore their advice. A long jacket only makes your legs look short. Instead stick to jackets that end on your hip bone.

* A coat is not just for Christmas. Always look for summer coats as well in lots of gorgeous fabrics. They will brighten up every outfit.

* If you possess trousers with any pockets, shred them now. Pockets add bulk wherever they are.

* Elaborate necklaces that start at your collar bone and fill your décolletage are your best friend for throwing the spotlight on your top half. Start collecting great pieces at markets and when you go on holiday.

* Avoid bare flesh at the neck. A wide scoop neck reduces your shoulder line. Narrow necklines are more flattering for your shape.

'IF YOU POSSESS
TROUSERS WITH
ANY POCKETS,
SHRED THEM NOW.
POCKETS ADD
BULK WHEREVER
THEY ARE'

✳ Collect bright scarves and
use them at every opportunity
to attract attention and bring
colour to your top half.

BELLS
TO INSPIRE YOU...

WE ROAMED the red carpets from London to LA and hunted the pages of Heat and Hello! looking for celebrity role models of the Bell persuasion. Dear reader, we have to be frank, they were thin on the ground and those we did encounter were mostly dressing appallingly for their body shape.

Your Bell shape does not come upon you until later in life, after childbirth at the earliest and sometimes only with the onset of menopause. Sadly, the media is not as obsessed with older women as they are with the young nubile variety. So we have found it hard to find celebrities for you to identify with.

Yet if you are looking for a role model, who could be more inspiring than the woman who may well become the first female President of the most powerful empire in modern times?

Hillary Clinton

✓ Photograph after photograph of Hillary showed her wearing this look. While we can't agree with the length of the jacket, the small, high lapels certainly focus our attention on her shoulders. Her trousers are a good, wide cut. So flattering on her thighs and bottom.

✗ If you are a Bell shape, you will only make matters worse by wearing a dress shaped like a Christmas tree, a pagoda... or a giant bell.

The Vase

*'People find my figure sexy, but
I sometimes just feel frumpy'*

Big tits

*Gently curving
longer waist*

Hips equal tits

Slim thighs and legs

The Vase
YOUR SHAPE

TAKE AN HOURGLASS and stretch her a bit and there you are – a Vase is born. You are an easier shape to dress than an Hourglass because you don't go in and out so much, and you have a flatter bottom. But Susannah, a classic Vase, feels differently. And a lot of you are of the same view.

You feel that your boobs are disproportionately large and your tummy has an amoeba-like ability to change shape every few seconds. You aren't thrilled about the size of your arms either. You put clothes on and you feel fat. Fat because your tits get in the way and fat because your arms don't allow for sleeveless tops. What makes matters worse is that no one sympathises. They still see the Playboy bunny. Even if you are a large Vase, you still have the proportions of a seriously sexy woman.

Sexy is all well and good, but it can often be hard to translate into style. You might get told that you have a great body, but it's not one that can easily be up-to-the-minute trendy.

Styles for you are specific. Sharp, tight tailoring… Miss Moneypenny on Viagra is your ideal look. Keep that in mind as your blueprint. Size definitely is not an issue here. Your proportions are fabulous and the saucy secretary look can easily be adapted to any dimensions.

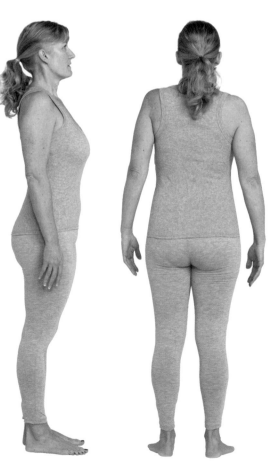

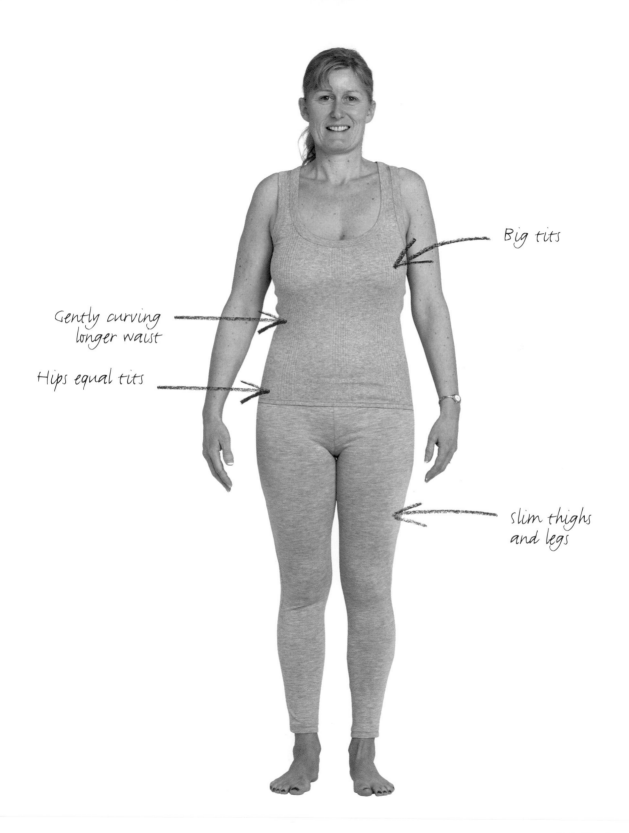

Big tits

Gently curving
longer waist

Hips equal tits

slim thighs
and legs

The Vase
YOUR BIGGEST MISTAKES

A VASE IS SUPPOSED to be shapely and elegant. Anything smock-like will hang from your tits, allowing enough room for a litter of puppies to be stashed away inside. To put it another way, you look pregnant.

A Vase will often have a disproportionately small face, so high necks and ruffles will make your boobs balloon in comparison to the size of your head.

Your upper arms tend not to be your best feature either, so it is wise to keep them covered.

Your slim legs, however, are another one of your fabulous assets, but boat-like shoes such as these make your feet seem bigger and your legs ungainly.

Never wear
Ruffles around your neckline
Dresses or skirts with tiered frills
Sleeveless round-neck tops
Polo-neck jumpers
Princess collars
Wedge shoes

'ANYTHING SMOCK-LIKE... WILL MAKE YOU LOOK PREGNANT'

The Vase
KEY SHAPES

Jacket

The single button should fasten between just under the boobs and your waist, no lower. This will draw all the emphasis to the narrowest part of your torso, just where your ribs end. The very open lapel cuts your boob area in half while the curve of the lapel echoes your womanly shape, adding a feminine touch so you don't have to reach for the ruffles.

Dress

The wide, scooped neckline helps to balance your chest with the rest of your body. Never wear any ribbing on your boobs. The ribbing on this dress emphasises the narrow part under your bust. Wearing fabrics that have shimmer or fleck is great way to be eye-catching without turning yourself into a potted plant.

Shirt

The puffed sleeve of this shirt takes the emphasis away from your tits. Make sure your shirts are fitted at the waist. If you want to wear a shirt untucked, make sure it ends at the top of your hips and has a curved hemline. This will veil your flabby tummy and highlight your shapely hips.

Skirt

A pencil skirt encompasses your shape, lifting and hugging your bottom and nipping into your waist. It should end at the narrowest part of your knee – that is to say, just below it.

Top

Your best assets are up top so spend your effort on great tops that will last you for years and make the most of your figure. The principles of this top are key. The low, squarish neckline divides up your body, and the cropped sleeve shows off your slim forearm, drawing the talking point down and away from your boobs.

Trousers

You can afford to wear pockets in the side of your trousers, so long as they are at a slant in front of your hips and not at the side, where they might pull. Wearing a big belt in the belt loops suits you and gives a bit of support for your tummy.

Dress

A dress that is based on a heavily structured frame holds your body in a film star shape while draping and gathers soften your outline.

Jeans

You don't have the snake hips required for skinny jeans, but your slim pins will look fabulous in true straight leg jeans.

Earrings

Generally, accessories should echo the shape you are. What's good about these earrings is that they are round. You don't suit angular jewellery.

Shoes

You're a curvy girl and you need a curvy shoe. Your slim ankles could easily be overwhelmed by a wedge.

Single button jacket with rounded lapel

Scooped-neck knit dress, fitted under boobs

Fitted shirt with puffed sleeves

High-waisted pencil skirt

Top with square neckline and cropped sleeve

Trousers with slanted pockets and big belt loops

Hold-it-all-in glamorous dress

Straight leg jeans

Rounded earrings

Curvy peep-toe shoes

The Vase
YOUR BEST LOOK
CASUAL

YOU CAN WEAR jeans until the cows come home. Beware of being seen in them so often that you give the impression that your life is just sitting around waiting for those old cows...

Like your sister the Hourglass, you look your best when you raise the stakes. Learn how to ramp up your jeans by wearing them in the same way you would wear smart trousers. Try them with a coat instead of a jumper, a shirt instead of a top. Your outfit then becomes one that will take you right through the day. You need two pairs of jeans in your wardrobe, one pair to wear with heels and another to wear with flats.

With big boobs, it's quite easy to feel a bit plump. So it's important that your clothes pay attention to your more dainty body parts. The first impression we get here is of Helen's very delicate wrists and hands and her slim, shapely legs. This is the outfit you wear when you don't want your tits totally on display.

The back of the coat is very fitted with a big button to draw it in under the boobs and give shape to the back. A slim coat with three-quarter sleeves is a very different proposition to a coat with big sleeves, belts and multiple fastenings. It means you can wear it indoors, like a jacket, without feeling that someone may be hovering nearby, ready to say: 'Would you like me to take your coat, madam?'

It's important for you to avoid floaty, chiffony things with too much print, but it's also important to always have something in your outfit that adds a touch of femininity. A great way to create interest without getting too patterned is to choose a fabric that has a subtle stripe, fleck or tone-on-tone design. This shirt has a blue-on-blue pattern that lifts the outfit without obscuring you.

'LEARN TO
WEAR YOUR
JEANS IN THE
SAME WAY
YOU WOULD
WEAR SMART
TROUSERS'

The Vase
YOUR BEST LOOK
SMART

THIS OUTFIT shows off your great lower legs and enhances your curves in all the right ways, while hiding the flabbyish tummy and upper arms that you don't care to show. In disguising the bits you don't like, you haven't compromised on making the most of the bits that we all love.

You will often find a great shirt that fits you on the boobs but is too big around the middle. A great solution to this problem is to invest in a sleeveless tank top. It lifts and separates, shows off the shirt and keeps your figure slim by sucking in under your boobs and around your little waist (see Recycle Your Wardrobe on page 241 for a great tip on creating tank tops from old jumpers).

Your femininity is all there courtesy of your curvy outline. The use of extraneous lace, ruffles, flowers, beads or baubles would only distract from that. This outfit uses sharp tailoring to create shape and support for your bum and tum, with feminine softness added in the sleeves.

Keep it simple. Your shoes echo this principle with their rounded shape, peep toes and a big but plain bow.

'THIS OUTFIT USES SHARP TAILORING TO CREATE SHAPE AND SUPPORT FOR YOUR BUM AND TUM WITH FEMININE SOFTNESS ADDED IN THE SLEEVES'

The Vase
YOUR BEST LOOK PARTY

YOUR CHARACTER might be drawn to floral and feminine dresses, but it's the worst look for you. A cascade of frills and floaty froth will do you no favours so blinker your eyes when shopping in that particular department.

Your perfect dress should cling to your bottom, breasts and waist like a love-starved barnacle. It should be made in a fabric that is heavy enough to support your curves and at the same time hold you all in place. Avoid diaphanous or slinky materials.

You suit a square-cut neckline more than a deep V, because the more breadth you show, as opposed to depth, the better proportioned your boobs will be to the rest of your body.

While this neckline shows off your boobs to their best advantage, a little puff sleeve takes the emphasis upwards, giving our eyes somewhere to rest other than your cleavage.

With a dress this structured it's important that your shoes aren't too delicate. They need to maintain a balance between your large chest and your slim legs, that is, the heels need to be sturdy enough so that you don't look as if you are about to topple over, but not so sturdy that they overwhelm your delicate ankle. No platforms for you; these are the perfect compromise.

'YOUR PERFECT DRESS SHOULD CLING TO YOUR BOTTOM, BREASTS AND WAIST LIKE A LOVE-STARVED BARNACLE'

WHAT IT MEANS TO BE A VASE

* As a Vase you carry your weight at the front of your body, so when temperatures are soaring, avoid fabrics and colours that go dark if you tend to perspire.

* Jeans suit you so well. Make sure they are fitted and try to have more than one pair in your wardrobe.

* Your body is born to run and to swim. Keep it in good condition.

* For country walks, get yourself a pair of boots with a rubber heel or small wedge. Flat shoes and boots are not your style. And invest in a fitted outdoors jacket, never a Barbour or a Puffa.

* Keep your hairstyle long and/or full so that your head doesn't look small in comparison to your big boobs and chunky upper arms.

* A structured halter neck bikini with wide straps will do wonders for your confidence at the beach.

* You're a curvy girl who needs curvy accessories. Choose a rounded, soft bag in preference to a hard, square block. This applies to jewellery too – look for rounded, not square or angular, pieces.

'YOU'RE
A CURVY
GIRL WHO
NEEDS CURVY
ACCESSORIES'

VASES
TO INSPIRE YOU...

Kate Winslet

✔ This is the way to knock 'em dead. Take one curvy Vase figure, suck it into a hugging, sculpting column of a dress with wide, supportive straps, a perfect bra, and panelling to hold in the tummy, minimise the waist and hug the bottom. Top it all off with the stunning smile of Kate Winslet. It's a winner every time.

✗ Like her sister the Hourglass, a Vase-shaped woman is overwhelmed in head-to-toe black. Here the polo neck enlarges the size of Kate's bust and the effect is enhanced by a not-very-supportive bra shining through too-sheer fabric. This outfit does nothing to show off Kate's waspy waist and curvaceous figure.

Kelly Brook

✓ The cut of this dress accentuates all the curves of Kelly's gorgeous body. A cut-out keyhole breaks up her chest and shows a flash of cleavage without being in your face, while the puffed sleeves mean that her cleavage isn't the only place we rest our eyes. The small, regular print is about the most pattern that a Vase should ever wear. Peep-toed shoes are just too cute to be legal.

✗ If you were suffering in the resentful belief that Kelly Brook would look fabulous in just anything, then here's your soothing balm. This dress does nothing to support her boobs whilst the spacing of the stripes only makes those knockers look enormous. What's more, it's a terrible length, even on her wonderful legs.

Geena Davis

✓ This is a wonderful dress for a Vase. The neckline and shoulders are cut to give great proportions to Geena Davis's top and the gold band under the bust emphasises her little waist. The skirt shows off her curvy shape and elongates her legs. Vases need strong shapes and the simple blocks of colour in this dress really work.

✗ What's even worse than a polo neck for making a Vase's upper body look mis-shapen? A sleeveless polo neck! This white monstrosity makes Geena appear hunched and lumpy up top while her gorgeous legs, entombed all in black, have become almost invisible.

The
Brick

*'I know I have a shape somewhere,
but I can't seem to find it'*

Broad shoulders

No waist

Average tummy

Flat bum

Chunky thighs

Chunky calves

The Brick
YOUR SHAPE

OH BOY! THE BRICK. You might think, can't we come up with another name? But this brings to life the challenges of your shape.

Your predicament is that from behind you have a masculine shape. A boyish flat bum, no waist, straight up and down legs and broad shoulders that would come in very handy if you were in an Olympic swimming team. You look powerful and strong, which is wonderful in the gym, but not so lovely at a time when you want people to see your fragile side. And there's a good chance that your clothes reflect your masculine lines too.

You no doubt feel it's impossible to be feminine, and you are right, it's hard. But the thing you can do in spades is glamour. Look at Kim Cattrall or Jennifer Hudson – real Brick babes! They are alluring, charismatic and filled with confidence in the knowledge that they have turned their geometric shape into something way beyond sensual.

We cannot stress how much we want you to take on board our advice in this chapter. Do so and, more than any other shape, your transformation will be profound.

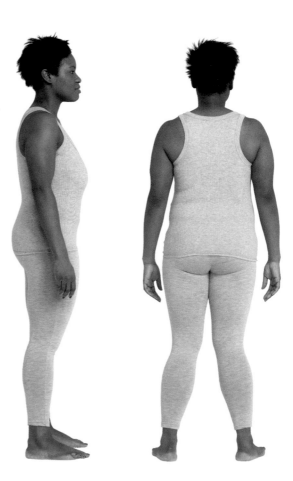

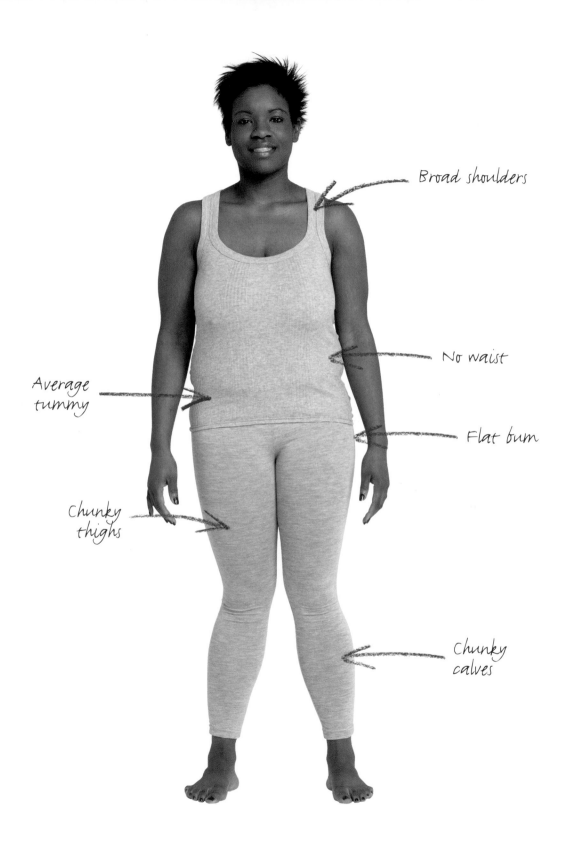

Broad shoulders

No waist

Average
tummy

Flat bum

Chunky
thighs

Chunky
calves

The Brick
YOUR BIGGEST MISTAKES

THE THINGS THAT YOU LOOK most utterly ghastly in are short skirts that snare the widest part of your thigh, and straight up and down tops that hit the same leg spot over formless trousers or – even more unspeakable – a long amorphous skirt.

If you sometimes feel that it's de rigueur to wear boots with the mini skirt, then on those occasions you really ought to be spread with wet concrete and added to a new apartment block building.

Anything square, like unstructured t-shirts or boxy jackets, will mirror your perpendicular body, leaving you no possibility of working the all-important art of magical illusion.

Never wear
Boxy jackets
Double breasted coats
Mini skirts
Box pleats
Trousers in stiff fabric
Heavy, solid wedge shoes

'YOU MUST NEVER WEAR SHORT SKIRTS THAT SNARE THE WIDEST PART OF YOUR THIGH'

The Brick
KEY SHAPES

Jacket

Most jackets over-emphasise the Brickiness of your shape. Even one-button jackets square up your body. Look for a jacket which fastens with a tie belt or sash to create a waist and yet shows off enough of what's underneath to break up the square of your torso.

Dress

The high waist of this wrap dress is a very flattering shape for the Brick as it draws attention to the one place of definition in your body. A rounded neckline opens up and separates your chest.

Top

The sequinned band reinforces the feminine roundedness of the neckline. Bricks need decoration, but it must be strong and graphic to avoid seeming ineffectual against your shape. A block of sequins achieves this.

Asymmetric skirt

The asymmetrical inset pleats on this skirt give the illusion of the lower body going in and out. They also lift and caress your bottom.

Vest

A fitted tank top carves into your figure. If you have dodgy arms, wear it over a shirt or with a fitted shrug. Keep the shrug short enough to show off your waist so it will look smaller in comparison to the width of the shrug.

Draping top

The way this top cleverly drapes under the boobs gives an illusion of flowing movement.

Coat

The empire line of this coat nips in your waist and skims over your tum and bum, adding curves to your shape.

Trousers

The Brick requires flop in her trousers. Avoid linen and harder fabrics that won't do anything for your shape. Instead, go for trousers that flow, like these jersey sweat pants. The hardness created by zips and buttons is removed, thus allowing your trousers to act as a backdrop to the main event going on upstairs.

Panelled skirt

The weight of a beaded or sequinned skirt will flatten your tum while the inset panels give soft, flowing movement as you walk.

Shoes

Bricks need curves and this should extend to your shoes too. A curved heel and rounded toe in a chunky shape looks great with your silhouette. Brick-like shoes will only make you seem too chunky, whereas spindly heels won't carry your frame.

Tie belt jacket

High wrap dress

Round neckline top with graphic decoration

Asymmetric skirt

Fitted tank top

Draping jersey top

Empire-line coat

Floppy trousers

Sequinned panelled skirt

Chunky, curvy shoes

The Brick
YOUR BEST LOOK
CASUAL

YOUR OUTLINE IS SOLIDLY straight-up-and-down so we need to show you as many tricks as possible to conjure up curves out of nowhere. Stripes can be quite magical. In uniform horizontal bands they tend to flatten and widen a body, but vary the widths and spacing of the stripes and – voilà – they start creating all sorts of strange optical illusions.

Here the wide central stripe gives the suggestion of a waist while the band running from the shoulder, around the neckline and down the front of Sabrina's cardigan accentuates her shapely bust and reduces the width of her middle. A great bra lifts the breasts upward and outward.

Your wide thighs make it very difficult for you to find trousers that fit. You must never wear your trousers too tight as they will only show off the parts you love to hate. Instead, look out for a pair of trousers with super-wide legs and wear them with large wedge shoes hidden underneath like a pair of concealed stilts. Wide, relaxed sweat pants look great on you, but the fabric must be thick enough to prevent any tell-tale cellulite showing through.

'WE NEED TO
SHOW YOU AS
MANY TRICKS
AS POSSIBLE
TO CONJURE UP
CURVES OUT
OF NOWHERE'

The Brick
YOUR BEST LOOK SMART

WHEN IT COMES TO straight lines, just say no. Follow instead the curvy path through life. Look for curved seams, sweetheart necklines, patterns that accentuate and decrease, curvy jewellery and curvy handbags. Everything here is working, working again and then working some more to create those precious curves.

The tank top bites into your torso, carving an hourglass out of a square. Worn alone, the white shirt would make you appear boxy in the body. Remember always to allow knitted tops to fall in gentle folds at your waist, rather than pulling them down to create another rigid shape.

It's vital that you only ever show off the lower half of your legs, keeping our eyes firmly diverted from the thickening going on above your knees. The asymmetric gores in this skirt create a sweeping curve across the front of your legs. When you walk down the street, this skirt will swish back and forth in such a way that passers-by will swear blind that they just saw a mermaid sashaying down to the bus stop.

And even the shoes are curvy.

'EVERYTHING
HERE IS
WORKING…
TO CREATE
THOSE
PRECIOUS
CURVES'

The Brick
YOUR BEST LOOK
PARTY

HERE'S ANOTHER TRICK. Clever patterns can create a curvaceous figure. The way that the print on this dress varies in size and intensity gives an illusion of shading around your waist. The diaphanous fabric is very feminine, but contrasting that with a strong animal print is a clever way to stop it from being too fairy tale for your frame. We just love the use of a small ruffle to emphasise and soften your boobs.

Because the dress ends above the knee, short dark leggings are needed to shape your legs. They act like a giant shadow, reducing the appearance of your knees and thereby giving an exaggerated curve to your calf.

'THE WAY THAT THE PRINT ON THIS DRESS VARIES IN SIZE AND INTENSITY GIVES AN ILLUSION OF SHADING AROUND YOUR WAIST'

WHAT IT MEANS TO BE A BRICK

* Stripes can work well for you. Don't wear a Dennis the Menace top – that will only broaden you. But varying the pace of stripes creates an optical illusion of curviness.

* Drapey fabrics are great for creating gathers, knots and swirly movement.

* Ditch the hoody and jeans. They make you look like a bloke. For casual moments you can wear wide-leg sweat pants, but always shape your top half.

* Have a drawer full of long silky scarves. These are really handy to break up your top and keep warm at the same time.

* For work, the best way to wear a classic white shirt is with a figure-sculpting, scoop-necked tank top over it.

* Three-quarter length sleeves really feminise your shape. They show off the more delicate parts – your wrists, hands and forearms.

* On the beach avoid a kaftan, it's too square making. Instead, look for a long chiffon robe that you can wear with a belt to give yourself shape.

* Winter is a difficult time for you. Thick fabrics and layering really add to your Brickiness. Look for jackets and coats with wide lapels that go out almost to your shoulder, but make sure they sweep right down to your sternum to break up the chest. Then add a big belt to winch in your waist.

* If wearing a classic mac, don't do up the buttons and then neatly fasten the belt. Instead, tie that belt as tight as heaven permits to winch in your waist.

'THREE-
QUARTER
LENGTH
SLEEVES
WILL
FEMINISE
YOUR
SHAPE'

BRICKS
TO INSPIRE YOU...

Dame Judi Dench

✓ The low, shapely diamond neckline gives more curve to Dame Judi Dench's upper half than the straight V variety would. The robe creates a pool of fabric at Dame Judi's feet that is wider than her shoulders, thus making them look smaller.

✗ There is a danger that comes with wearing full-length cover-ups – one wrong turn and you're in tent city. The King of Morocco's tent city, at that.

Jennifer Hudson

✔ Sweeping all the fabric up into a central knot directs our attention to the centre of Jennifer's waist and at the same time creates soft gathers that allow movement around her butt and thighs. The shape of the bodice and neckline make her bust look a lot more neat and uplifted than it otherwise might.

✖ This dress is cut on the bias so the fabric clings mercilessly to Jennifer's rear. The diagonal bands on her boobs have the effect of spreading the bust outwards and then downwards at the sides, making her breasts seem completely unmanageable.

Kim Cattrall

✔ Being flat-chested means one can get away with a navel-skimmingly deep neckline and our Kim is milking it for all it's worth. All the lines of this dress converge fabulously in a knotted waistband at the centre of her torso, thus creating a sexy S shape. The skirt swishes around her slightly chunky calf, making it seem more slender and shapely. And her shoes are low cut, elongating Kim's legs.

✖ A strapless style gives a square shape to Kim's top half, exaggerating the Brickiness of her physique. Cutting out a window at the waist just clearly shows that she hasn't got one.

The
Lollipop

'I've got enormous knockers, and life was difficult growing up, but I've learned to live with them'

Big tits

Slight waist

Slim hips

Long legs

The Lollipop
YOUR SHAPE

WHEN WE WERE researching celebrity body shapes for this book, we noticed how many of the world's most glamorous movie stars were Lollipops. With your buxom boobs and endless legs you are most men's idea of sex on a stick, the female equivalent of a Ferrari. Yet you can feel surprisingly ungainly and unconfident at times. On the red carpet nobody can beat your form, but let's face it, how many acres of crimson Wilton do they roll out in the supermarket car park or by the banks of the local duck pond?

While evening gowns are generally made in Lollipop heaven, regular daywear can be more problematic. Too-short sleeves, too-tight tops and high-waisted trousers can make you look like Bambi on a bad day – all uncoordinated legs and arms flying about the place. Your shoulders are not broad enough to support your bosoms with ease, so you have a tendency to collapse into a hunch. You really need to pay attention to your posture at all times. Being short-waisted only adds to that top-heavy impression.

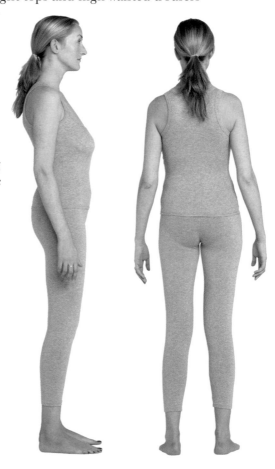

That said, once you learn the art of balancing your silhouette, we assure you that you can be one of the most knockout women around – whether it be at a gala first night or the school play. Read on, dear Lollipop...

'WITH YOUR BUXOM BOOBS AND ENDLESS LEGS YOU ARE... THE FEMALE EQUIVALENT OF A FERRARI'

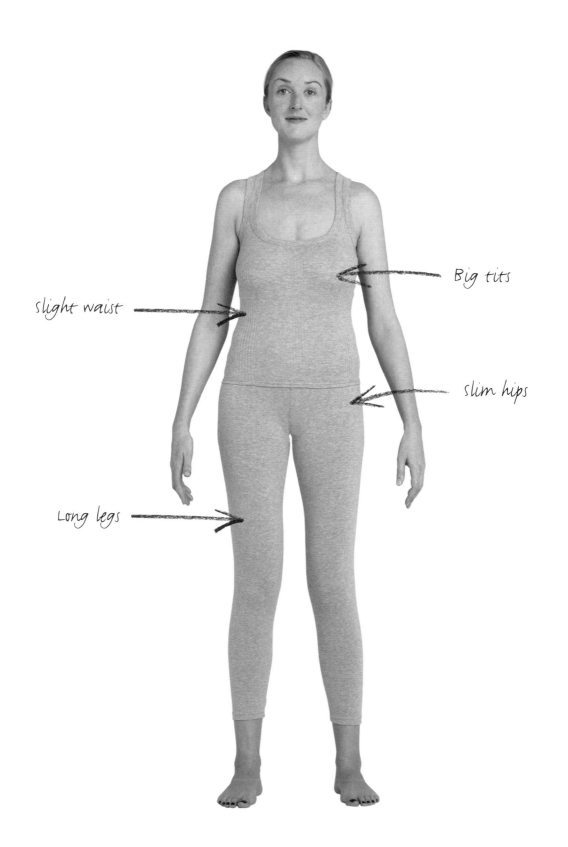

Big tits

slight waist

slim hips

Long legs

The Lollipop
YOUR BIGGEST MISTAKES

YOU HAVE ALWAYS been told you have fabulous legs, and indeed you do. Long, lean and lithe, they are the envy of all your friends.

When you dress, you do so to make the most of your best asset. High-waisted jeans and trousers are a favourite. They make your pins look endless, but the rest of you is then compressed to the point that your head appears barely over the top of your waistband. When your legs are on display, where is the rest of you? High-cut trousers and polo-neck sweaters turn you into an exaggerated version of yourself. Not the 'girl with the long legs', just 'the long, long legs'.

You must remember and honour your bust, which is a part of your wonderful form. Don't let your breasts sink to your waist or allow them to hang from your chin with throat-throttling necklines. Cropped jackets and ballooning shift dresses must be added to your list of no-nos.

Never wear
Polo necks
Chunky sweaters
High-waisted trousers
Shift dresses that
  hang from your tits
Bolero jackets
Elaborate necklaces

'HIGH-CUT TROUSERS AND POLO-NECK SWEATERS TURN YOU INTO AN EXAGGERATED VERSION OF YOURSELF'

'YOUR FABULOUS LEGS ARE THE ENVY OF ALL YOUR FRIENDS'

The Lollipop
KEY SHAPES

Coat

It's important that the buttons on this coat sit underneath your boobs. Buttons on your tits would act like a couple of targets, but in this way the buttons draw attention to your waist. The coat then swoops outward, suggesting fuller hips beneath.

Top

A tank top is a great device to enable you to wear a shirt. It contains the shirt and stops it hanging from your boobs. Your outline is now shapely, rather than tent-like.

Jacket

Double buttons under the boobs lengthen your waist, while a busy print breaks up the expanse of your chest.

Draping skirt

This jersey skirt gathers on the hip, creating a sexy drape that exaggerates the swish of your hips as you walk. Drapey fabrics are wonderful for giving fluidity to your shape.

Trousers

Wide bell-bottom trousers balance out your boobs so you look less top heavy.

Bikini

A structured halter neck with wide straps is great for bust containment and support, while boy shorts exaggerate your hips.

Top

A wide sweetheart neckline is absolutely the most flattering on you. It reduces the expanse of your bust and then nips back into your neck, thereby broadening your shoulders.

Fluted skirt

A fluted skirt with its flaring hemline helps to balance your top half and create the illusion of hip movement.

Dress

Strategic knots and gathers will direct all eyes to the centre of your waist. Fine jersey is great for creating twisting, sinuous shapes.

Shoes

Your shoes should be slim heeled to reflect your slim legs, yet straight enough to give a feeling of support to your top half.

Coat with full skirt and buttons
under boobs

Scoop neck tank top

Print jacket
with double buttons

Halter neck bikini
with boy shorts

Skirt with hip detail

Bell-bottom trousers

Knotted and gathered
jersey dress

Top with wide sweetheart
neckline

Fluted skirt

Slim, straight-heeled shoes

The Lollipop
YOUR BEST LOOK
CASUAL

YOU'RE ALL TITS and legs. While that may be many people's idea of heaven, those people are mostly men. The truth is that when you're on form and everything's working well you look and feel like the most fabulous chick on the block, but when your clothes sit badly you can feel surprisingly awkward and self-conscious.

What you aim to achieve with your clothes is to broaden your hips and shoulders and create fluid shapes in your body. Think of a long 'S' shape rather than a giant 'P'. The volume of the shirt sleeves and the width of the bell-bottom trousers both conspire to make your waist appear smaller, thus giving more shape to the hips.

The corseting effect of the waistcoat elongates your waist, making your body seem more in balance with your legs.

A wide sweetheart neckline is the ultimate shape for broadening shoulders and giving you an instant breast reduction.

'YOU SHOULD AIM
TO BROADEN YOUR HIPS
AND SHOULDERS AND
CREATE FLUID SHAPES
IN YOUR BODY'

The Lollipop
YOUR BEST LOOK PARTY

IT IS DIFFICULT for a Lollipop to wear a dress. Dresses can kill your figure unless finely tuned to power up your weak areas.

Your floorboard waist must always be balanced by a flared hemline that kicks out, flitting away from your knee. Your boobs will only benefit from a wide neckline that lifts and separates those orbs skywards, thus elongating your waist and giving a curve to your upper body.

Make sure that your dress fits you beautifully on the tits and then get it taken in at the waist, if necessary. Like your sisters, the Brick and the Goblet, your silhouette benefits greatly from soft, drapey dresses that gather into the centre of your body. This trick unfailingly swoops our eye to that critical middle point, making your waist seem smaller and your hips wider.

Shoes with slim but straight heels do wonders for balancing your boobs without being too heavy for your long legs.

'YOUR SILHOUETTE BENEFITS GREATLY FROM SOFT, DRAPEY DRESSES THAT GATHER INTO THE CENTRE OF YOUR BODY'

WHAT IT MEANS
TO BE A LOLLIPOP

* Most high street stores simply don't do bikinis that will fit top and bottom. Bravissimo has a great range of stylish bikinis with big cup sizes and you can choose the tops and bottoms separately.

* When you do find a bikini that fits, treasure it. Salt water, sun and chlorine all attack the lycra, so wash and rinse your bikini by hand each night then hang it out and it will be dry in the morning.

* Your shoulders are not really broad enough to support your big boobs so beware of slouching. A simple reminder when you're sitting on the bus or train is to put a dot on your watch hand. Every time you see that dot, draw your stomach in and shoulders back. Imagine the invisible centred line stretching up through your core and out through the crown of your head.

* When you find a pair of trousers that are long enough, buy two pairs.

* As you get older you will tend to put on weight around your tummy. It may not be much but on a frame as slim as yours, it will show. Get a good regime of sit-ups and abdominal exercises in place early in life. This will stand you in good stead as you reach your fifties. If you're nearing or past your fifties, it's never too late – start today.

* Things that will broaden your shoulders without adding to your tits: balloon sleeves, shoulder pads, puff sleeves, narrow lapels.

* Your swan-like neck is a wonderful asset. Start moisturising it morning and night.

✳ Collect really great corsets and fitted waistcoats to wear over all your shirts and some of your summer dresses, too. Look in vintage stores and charity shops for unexpected treasures.

✳ When you're on form you are the sexiest shape in the pack, but you can equally feel horribly self-conscious. Remember that covering up will not make you disappear. Work out some fall-back outfits that you always feel comfortable in and take Polaroids of yourself wearing them. On down days you will lack the inspiration to create those outfits, so this will be a useful aide-memoire.

'WHEN YOU'RE ON FORM YOU ARE THE SEXIEST SHAPE IN THE PACK...'

LOLLIPOPS
TO INSPIRE YOU...

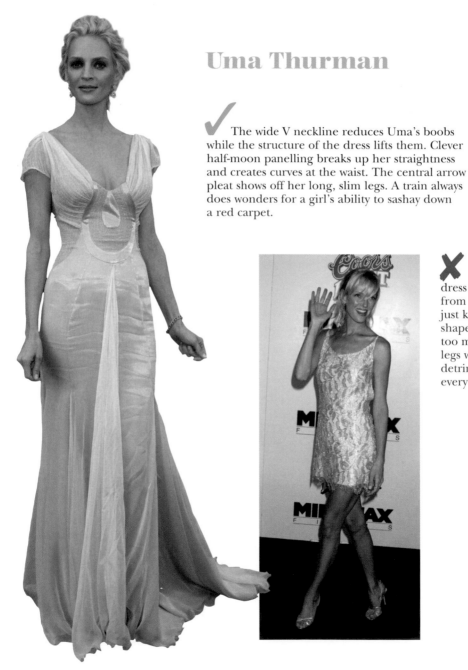

Uma Thurman

✔ The wide V neckline reduces Uma's boobs while the structure of the dress lifts them. Clever half-moon panelling breaks up her straightness and creates curves at the waist. The central arrow pleat shows off her long, slim legs. A train always does wonders for a girl's ability to sashay down a red carpet.

✗ A silver mini dress hanging from Uma's tits just kills their shape. Relying too much on her legs works to the detriment of everything else.

Susan Sarandon

✓ This dress has fishtails, giving Susan Sarandon the silhouette of a mermaid. It reveals her inner Jessica Rabbit by shaping her bottom half. The draping sarong effect gives sexy movement by creating a curving wave around the hips.

✗ Lollipops don't need to wear vertical stripes, they're tall and slim enough already. They also don't need to wear baggy, high-necked, shiny shirts to make their top half look enormous.

Angelina Jolie

✓ Angelina Jolie is a classic Lollipop – tits on a stick. A deep-cut neckline is great for reducing her chest size while the way this dress wraps around her torso gives shape and definition to her waist.

✗ This dress offers no support for Angelina's boobs, but rather hangs from them, in the manner of a large silk sack.

The
Pear

'I feel most uncomfortable wearing a swimsuit because of my saddlebags and chunky calves'

Small tits

Long waist

Flat tummy

Saddlebags

Heavy legs

The Pear
YOUR SHAPE

WHEN IT COMES to weight distribution, the centre of your woes lies around your butt. Not your butt per se, but those ballooning thighs that bulge out to the side... your saddlebags... the ones you have never been able to get rid of, no matter how many hours you spent on the Stairmaster. Then, sweeping downwards, we come to your calves and ankles which don't have the definition you would like. B-u-m-m-e-r. Don't you loathe your genes for passing you the Pear card?

Many times you have yearned to wear a mini skirt, but shied away from it at the last minute or gone for it, only to have felt self-conscious and conspicuous. It's not that you are or were overweight. Indeed, Pears can be skinny little chickies like Trinny, but her thighs are also, to be honest, way bigger than the rest of her.

As we see it, the Pear has many, many redeeming qualities... all of them upstairs. The boobs won't be big, but they will be a tidy handful that can slip easily into delicate and strappy pretty tops. Your arms, bless them, are nearly always toned to the point of perfection. Dammit, your top half is hard to fault. Muscular back, tiny waist and a card-hard stomach make you one lucky girl. Go forth and display your wares upstairs keeping the basement dark and mysterious to the outside world.

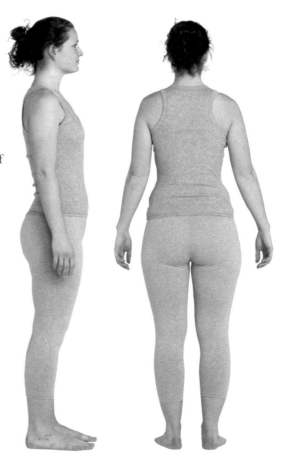

'THE PEAR HAS MANY, MANY REDEEMING QUALITIES... ALL OF THEM UPSTAIRS'

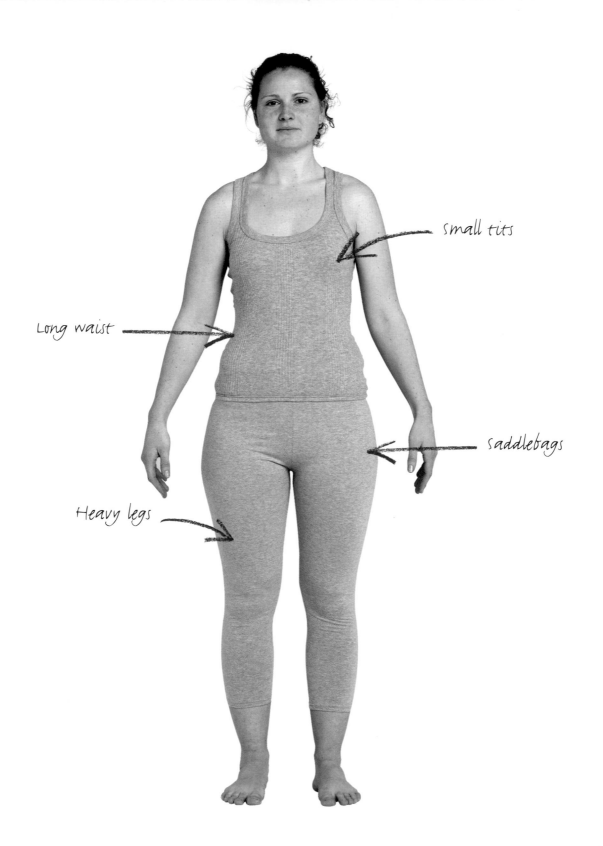

small tits

Long waist

saddlebags

Heavy legs

The Pear
YOUR BIGGEST MISTAKES

PSST! LOOKING FOR a pound of flesh? Then look no further than a Pear who went out and bought herself a mini dress! You simply must not bare your legs above the knee.

There are all sorts of tricks to aid in the artful presentation of your pins: long shorts, flared skirts, wide-leg trousers and leggings; but never, never naked legs with mini skirts.

This heinous crime is further compounded by the use of ankle straps, a hideous form of leg-shortening device once used in Victorian fashion dungeons.

Anything that draws attention to your lower half is a definite no-no.

Never wear
Bias-cut skirts
Pencil skirts
Skinny jeans
Jodphurs
Ankle straps
Stilettos

'YOU SIMPLY MUST NOT BARE YOUR LEGS ABOVE THE KNEE'

The Pear
KEY SHAPES

Shrug

You always need clever ways to broaden your shoulders and attract attention to your top half. When wearing a vest or a t-shirt, a glamorous shrug is the perfect device.

Jacket

You need a fabulous jacket to direct attention to your top half. Blinging silver does the trick.

Shirt

You are quite flat-chested so pretty, delicate fabrics add femininity to your figure. The puffed sleeves extend the line of your shoulder while the lighter inserts also increase their perceived size. This is a perfect shirt for a Pear.

Skirt

A great alternative to trousers for covering a Pear's legs. A long A-line skirt will be your best friend in the summer months.

Coat

Worn open, the line of your coat slices your thigh vertically. Belting your coat puts focus on your waist, allowing the bottom half to zoom out and unobtrusively cover your saddlebags.

Top

A shallow, slashed neckline widens the appearance of your shoulders, bringing them into balance with your hips. Interestingly, very narrow horizontal stripes set up an optical illusion that makes you look more curvy. A contrasting band at the hem of your top helps to shorten your long body and so makes your legs seem longer.

Dress

This is a wonderfully versatile dress for you. Wear it over a blouse or t-shirt for a daytime look or bare your shoulders in the evening. A strapless style broadens your shoulders while the flared skirt disguises your saddlebags.

Boots

In winter, straight boots are a godsend for covering the heft of those calves and allowing you to wear skirts and dresses.

Shoes

Straight heels and platforms work to minimise the chunkiness of your calves and ankles.

Trousers

Your trousers need to be wide enough in the leg to skim over saddlebags. Avoid side pockets and go for a flat front.

Shoulder-enhancing shrug

Eye-popping jacket

Delicate shirt with
puffed sleeves

Long A-line skirt

Boat neck top with
contrasting band on hemline

Belted coat

Strapless dress with full skirt

Straight boots

Chunky, straight heels
with platform

Wide-leg trousers
with flat front

The Pear
YOUR BEST LOOK
CASUAL

STAND TO ATTENTION, shoulders back! Well, that's a start. The name of the game is broadening your shoulders to balance those saddlebags. The era of the Dynasty-style padded power shoulder was a golden one for Pears – on the top half anyway. The less said about those four-inches-above-the-knee pencil skirts, the better.

You are relatively flat-chested so you can get away with higher cut tops than your busty Vase and Hourglass cousins. A slashed neckline always helps to give the impression of coathanger shoulders. Or, as Mel shows us here, an alternative way is to use puffed sleeves to add those vital inches.

Your legs are short in comparison to your body. Wearing layered tops, or in this case a short waistcoat layered over a longer top, helps to break up the length of your torso, thereby rebalancing your proportions. Hey, presto! Longer legs. Wearing trouser hemlines to the floor is essential to maximum leg extension.

Now let's look at your bottom half. The aim is to do everything possible to keep our attention away from those dreaded saddlebags. Tight, clingy trousers cause them to stick out like a pair of joke ears, so make sure that your trousers are wide enough and in a fabric that is heavy enough to skim right over your thighs.

Next, be sure that there are absolutely no side pockets to strain or bulge sideways. This pair has a tiny pocket detail at the waist instead to bring focus away from the saddlebags. Finally, your trousers should always be in the darkest colour of your outfit.

'THE NAME OF
THE GAME IS
BROADENING
YOUR
SHOULDERS
TO BALANCE
THOSE
SADDLEBAGS'

The Pear
YOUR BEST LOOK SMART

A STRAPLESS DRESS is a wonderful thing for a Pear to own. In the evening you can wear it with a drop dead gorgeous necklace to spotlight your top half and for daytime you can dress it down by wearing a t-shirt or full-sleeved blouse underneath. The stiff, flared skirt does a terrific job of disguising wide hips.

Straight boots below cover the chunkiness of your calf.

One of your main indulgences in life should be to start building a collection of amazing coats for every occasion and season. This is an investment for your future. We are not talking coats to keep off the rain and snow, or to protect you from brambles when out walking your dog; we mean coats that you can wear indoors or out in lieu of a jacket or, sometimes, can even be worn as a dress. Coats that have a narrow lapel to broaden your shoulders, coats that are fitted, with the main button sitting slightly above your waist, coats that are three-quarter or knee length to cover your saddlebags, coats that will accompany you throughout your life because they flatter your shape to perfection.

'ONE OF YOUR MAIN INDULGENCES IN LIFE SHOULD BE TO START BUILDING A COLLECTION OF AMAZING COATS FOR EVERY OCCASION AND SEASON'

'STRAIGHT
BOOTS
COVER THE
CHUNKINESS
OF YOUR
CALVES'

The Pear
YOUR BEST LOOK
PARTY

THIS OUTFIT COMBINES colour and texture to perfectly re-proportion your Pear shape and bring out the best of your features. The silhouette of the dress shows off your small waist and then flares out to disguise saddlebags, but the fabric is floaty enough so that it won't make you look as if you are about to blast off into the stratosphere.

The uneven, semi-transparent hem of the dress breaks up the line against the thickest part of your calf. The high, cross-over waistline makes your legs appear longer.

Most Pears are wider on their hips than their shoulders, so to broaden the top half wear a little sequinned shrug. It will also reflect added sparkle onto your face.

Your shoes should have straight heels to perfectly balance your overall look.

'HERE COLOUR AND TEXTURE PERFECTLY RE-PROPORTION YOUR PEAR SHAPE'

'A LITTLE
SEQUINNED
SHRUG WILL
BROADEN YOUR
TOP HALF AND
ADD SPARKLE
TO YOUR FACE'

WHAT IT MEANS TO BE A PEAR

✷ A fabulous push-up bra will give you the confidence to show off your trim top half for evening events.

✷ You may have a great summer party to go to, but if you've been on your feet all day you won't want to show off your ankles. Take 15 minutes to lie on the floor with your butt against the wall and your legs perpendicular. Let any puffiness gently drain away as you circle your feet twenty times in either direction.

✷ If you try on evening dresses that fit your waist and cover your saddle-bags, but make your top half look scrawny, remember that you can always wear a gilet or shrug to increase your shoulders.

✷ Things to make your top half look bigger: gilets, sequinned tops, faux fur wraps, big necklaces, puff sleeves, big earrings, layering.

✷ However big you are, a string bikini will reduce the appearance of your saddlebags and will elongate your legs as well.

✷ Set yourself free to wear skirts and dresses in the winter with a pair of the famous Hobbs boots. We recommend them to every Pear. They are long and straight with a two inch chunky heel (see page 229).

'REMEMBER
THAT YOU CAN
ALWAYS WEAR
A GILET OR
SHRUG TO
INCREASE
THE WIDTH
OF YOUR
SHOULDERS'

PEARS
TO INSPIRE YOU...

Shakira

✓ Shakira is young enough to expose a significant amount of skin on her chest. This plunging neckline really does a great job of pointing our line of vision in the right direction. The gathered-in waist emphasises the curviness of her torso and the skirt flips out just enough to skim her bum and saddle-bags. Bell-bottom trousers are great for balancing larger haunches, as are brick-like platform shoes.

✗ While the bright yellow top does grab our attention, it doesn't do anything to enhance Shakira's shape or to broaden her shoulders. The long boots cut her legs in half, leaving her thighs adrift like a couple of khaki pontoons.

Katie Holmes

✓ A long skirt with a tulle underskirt for added flair is the ultimate way to ensure that no fabric ever clings to the fleshier parts. Here Katie shows how it's done with élan. The strapless bustier spotlights her fabulous décolletage, ensuring that our eyes remain fixed firmly above her waistline.

✗ Here tightly fitting jeans merely emphasise the saddlebags, so that as Katie walks we see every distortion in the outline of her legs.

Sandra Bullock

✓ A puffball dress completely obliterates the saddlebags while showing off Sandra's small-framed upper body. Having small boobs, she will invariably have a toned back and fabulous shoulders. The straight-across neckline broadens her top half and draws attention to her best assets.

✗ Pears must above all avoid cut-on-the-bias dresses. The fabric is pulling and straining around those big hips. Frills running all over the place only wave a flag in the direction of Sandra's saddlebags.

RECYCLE YOUR WARDROBE

ONE OF THE FEW adverse effects of reading this book is that you may now be seized with a desire to rush out and buy yourself a completely new wardrobe to suit your body shape.

This is not a course of action that we recommend. Your understanding of the principles that apply to your body shape will grow slowly as you try out different outfits and combinations and then come back again to this book.

We hope that having a thorough understanding of what works for your shape will help you to avoid many costly mistakes in the future, but we don't imagine that you will ever become a perfect paragon of self-knowledge and shopping efficiency.

As you have seen, we too have made some big mistakes in the past – and not just the dim and distant past. We still manage to fall into fashion traps more regularly than we would choose.

If you're like us, you will already have drawers and cupboards overflowing with seldom worn dresses, tops, trousers and skirts. Garments which have been bought and then sadly neglected because they are old, too big, almost big enough or they just never looked quite right when you got them home.

While we do love the look and feel of a designer shopping bag, we do not regard shopaholism as a positive lifestyle choice, rather as an affliction requiring daily vigilance to keep it under control.

Like everything else in life, shopping is all about moderation. One way to get the thrill of a new dress without releasing the ravening monster of throwaway consumerism is to recycle what you already have.

A trip to the dressmaker can be every bit as satisfying as a trip to Selfridges. That way you get to own clothes that are perfectly fitted to your figure and are truly unique. And you feel virtuous to boot.

WRONG COLOUR

Before

I fell utterly in love with the multi-layered draping neckline of this t-shirt, so I completely ignored the fact that it's 'nude' colour made me look as if I had spent the last fifteen months lying in a darkened hospital room. The end result? I never wore it.

Notes about dyeing

Dyes are notoriously temperamental, especially when it comes to synthetic and mixed fibres. Pure cotton is a safe bet. Mixed fibre fabrics might come out looking a bit patchy, but sometimes we quite like that. Synthetics like nylon or polyester will only absorb a little of the dye so the end result will be much paler than the shade on the packet.

It might sound obvious, but don't forget that if you boil-dye knits or silks they will shrink. Use cold-water dyes for all delicates.

Remember that you can't dye something a lighter shade than it originally was, neither should you expect pleasing results if dyeing opposing colours. For example, trying to renew a red garment with green dye will most likely result in a horrible sludgy brown.

Dyed garments must be washed separately forever more, otherwise you risk acquiring a complete set of pink/blue/purple sheets, towels, socks and pillowcases.

If it all goes horribly wrong and you end up throwing your old t-shirt or skirt in the bin, don't despair. You weren't wearing the damned thing anyway.

After

A quick go through the washing machine with a bottle of Jacquard acid dye transformed my previously unworn top into a ravishing new best friend. I love the way this colour zings my eyes.

FAVOURITE JUMPER HAS A HOLE IN IT

Before

Finding a jumper that is the perfect shape, length and colour is just heaven. The whole point of having a favourite jumper is to wear it all the time until it falls apart. Sadly, but inevitably, a hole appears at the wrist, armpit or elbow. At first I try to ignore it or I may claim that it's part of an intentional Boho look. Finally, as the hole grows and my denial recedes, I am forced to accept that my old trusty has had its day.

'FINALLY I AM FORCED TO ACCEPT THAT MY OLD TRUSTY HAS HAD ITS DAY'

How to hem knits

By hand, roll the edge and then blanket stitch, using normal sewing cotton. A stitch every 2mm should do the trick on an average weight jumper.

After
Cutting off the sleeves
and reshaping the neckline
means that my beloved
jumper can live again as
a flattering tank top.

EXPENSIVE MISTAKE

Before

The cost of this dress was sky high but the effect it had on me was most deflating. I emphasise on me because on another woman's body in this dress would have looked sensational. I had made the mistake of buying the dress as a work of art rather than as a garment whose sole purpose in life should be to make me look great.

A cut that would look sublime on a Lollipop just looked pointless on a Pear. The pleats on the bust made my chest look like a flat balloon, the waist was in the wrong place and the whole effect was of a very expensive potato sack. Yet I still loved the fabric...

After

Some minor changes made the dress much more flattering to my body shape. The pleats on the bust have been sewn down so that it's much more fitted, the hem has been taken up and adding elastic shirring has made the waist deeper. But then I realised that the real problem with this dress was that I hadn't figured out how to wear it. Adding a puff-sleeved shirt broadens my top half and makes my whole silhouette much more balanced. Adding a complementary belt breaks up the line of the dress and makes my waist look smaller. I'm so thrilled to have snatched victory from the jaws of defeat with this one.

'ADDING A PUFF-SLEEVED SHIRT BROADENS MY TOP HALF AND BALANCES MY PEAR SHAPE'

LOVE THE COLOUR, HATE THE SHAPE

Before

You know how it goes. You see an old 1980s dress in Oxfam. Suddenly you're struck by the realisation that you have discovered a wonderful treasure, the Rosetta Stone, the Ark of the Covenant of fashion. You sidle up to it, hoping that no one else will spot your precious gem before you have a chance to snatch it up and casually saunter to the till, praying now that the manager won't notice how seriously underpriced it is. 'Eight pounds? Sorry, madam, that should be £108.' Purchase made, you furtively rush home to parade about your bedroom in the new...hang on a minute, oh dear, that dress is just totally wrong. Well, you can always add it your collection of bright green silk dusters. Or...

After

The tummy pleats have been removed and the skirt re-cut to make an A-line, giving a much more svelte shape to my middle. Cutting and ruching the sleeves creates a flattering line at the tops of my arms. Adding sparkly stretch panels into the front and back of the dress covers my bra and gives the dress a modern look.

'ADDING SPARKLY STRETCH PANELS COVERS MY BRA AND FLATTERS MY VASE SHAPE'

TOO SHORT

Before

This t-shirt dress is absolutely the worst length for a Pear-shaped saddlebagger like me. It clings unlovingly to the widest part of my thigh and only enhances the chunkiness of my leg below. I don't know what I was thinking about when I bought it. Arrgh.

'THIS DRESS IS ABSOLUTELY THE WORST LENGTH FOR A PEAR-SHAPED SADDLEBAGGER LIKE ME'

After

Trusty scissors and sewing
machine have come to the
rescue yet again. By cutting
off a few inches at the bottom
and then gathering some of
the fabric in ruches at the sides
this t-shirt dress has become
the perfect shaped top for me
to wear with my ever-flattering,
wide-legged trousers.

BOXY JACKET

Before

Boxy jackets were very fashionable in the early 1960s so they can often be found in vintage shops made in wonderful period fabrics. Buying a jacket with the same quality of workmanship today would be prohibitively expensive. There's only one problem: this square-cut style isn't right for my body shape. It hangs from my tits, making me look like a little yellow marquee on the march across Britain.

'THIS SQUARE-CUT STYLE ISN'T RIGHT FOR MY BODY SHAPE... I LOOK LIKE A LITTLE YELLOW MARQUEE...'

After

Adding several darts into the back of the jacket has nipped it in at the waist and given it a kicking-out shape that makes the most of my Vase figure. Sewing a short, inverted pleat into the middle of the sleeve gives a wonderful curvy shape to my arm. It's a trick that Vivienne Westwood uses a lot.

BORED WITH IT

Before

This has been one of my favourite skirts. Its big bold pattern and long flared line is ideal for disguising my saddlebags so it has accompanied me to many, many summer parties, days out in the park and Mediterranean holidays. Consequently I've worn it so often that I'm now completely over it. But getting rid of this skirt after so much good service would be like sending a faithful old horse to the knackers' yard, so I've been thinking hard about how to give it a new lease of life...

'GETTING RID OF THIS SKIRT WOULD BE LIKE SENDING A FAITHFUL OLD HORSE TO THE KNACKERS' YARD...'

After

Reshaping the skirt gives it a new identity as a strapless dress. The waistband was let out to fit my bust and the back seam shaped to create a flattering line. A five inch piece cut from the hem provided a lovely long sash to tie around my waist. NB: short leggings are fantastic for giving shape to my legs and at the same time covering any sagginess in my knees. I wear them with any dress that is above knee length.

SHAPELESS SKIRT

Before
I was utterly seduced by the subtle silvery shimmer of the fabric in this skirt so it was easy to overlook the fact that it had about as much shape as a bin liner as I happily flashed the plastic. But as unflattering as it was, I still could not bear to throw it away.

'UNFLATTERING AS IT WAS, I STILL COULDN'T BEAR TO THROW IT AWAY...'

After

After administering a general anaesthetic, our dressmaker opened all the seams on this skirt. Then, using a much loved but long deceased skirt of mine as a pattern, she re-cut it into a pencil silhouette and shortened it by three or four inches.

It is worth saving old garments that fit you like a dream but have completely had their day – for moments just such as this.

TOO RETRO

Before

The quality of fabrics, prints and finishing in vintage clothes is far superior to the mass-produced high street clothes available now. Let's face it, even the priciest designer garments are manufactured for worldwide distribution so you will find pretty much the same thing on sale from London to Lima or Sydney to Shanghai.

Trawling through markets is one of my favourite pastimes. Spotting a beaded bodice or big floral print lurking on the rails is bound to get my sequinned heart skipping a beat faster. While the garments themselves are often gorgeous, the shapes of yesteryear don't necessarily flatter my figure. On top of that, silhouettes from the 1920s to the 1980s are distinctly of their time and wearing them today makes me feel that I'm on my way to a fancy dress party.

This dress has a spectacular print, but its skirt is too long, emphasising my chunky calves, the neckline is a touch low, thereby showing off my sun-ravaged décolleté, and the bodice is cut for those 1950s-style pointy breasts which I just don't have. It's altogether too retro.

After

Firstly, four inches was cut from the hem to make a more flattering length. Using that strip, our seamstress created a flat ruffle that was sewn in to create a new, higher neckline. Adding darts on the bodice made the dress more fitted to my shape. Finally, a designer belt gives it a contemporary finish. Some people would cry 'sacrilege' at the sight of us gleefully cutting and sculpting our vintage garments. Not us. When it comes to clothes, we want them to fit well and look great on us. We're not planning to open a fashion museum.

'WE WANT CLOTHES TO FIT WELL AND LOOK GREAT ON US – NOT FOR A FASHION MUSEUM'

OUR DIRECTORY

High Street Stores

Accessorize
Brilliant hats, bags, purses, scarves, sandals and jewellery – you can always find something in this wonderful shop!

All Saints
Slightly offbeat, hip styling, plenty of revealing evening outfits, very Boho. Cool distressed leather jackets, flimsy tops and complicated dresses – lovely, but best on skinny girls. Sizes 8–14.

American Apparel
Super-hip separates shop from the States. Cool hipster knickers in gold lamé and cotton, multitude of stretchy tanks, leggings, dresses – anything and everything in pretty much any colour jersey. Amazing hoodies and sweat pants. Sizes 6–16.

Arrogant Cat
Striking young fashions aimed mostly at party girls with great figures. Well worth a look though, as they do have some lovely things. Sizes 8–14.

Coast
Good for occasional and evening wear, very attractive designs. The window display is always eye-catching and they tend to be pretty adventurous with colours and styling. Good jackets and coats as well. Sizes 8–18.

Cos
A more upmarket version of H&M. Excellent high-fashion designs in muted colours, with echoes of Miu Miu and Marni. Wonderful accessories and underwear. Sizes 8–16.

Diesel
Fantastic jeans and sexy skirts if you have youth and a slim figure on your side. Think sexy gas station attendant. Underwear, sunglasses, bags and perfume also available. Sizes 8–14.

Dorothy Perkins
Funky fashionable separates and dresses up to size 20. So much to choose from that finding the gems can be difficult. Sizes 8–22 and 8–20 in the Petite range. Lingerie 34A–38D.

Evans
The only high street store truly dedicated to larger ladies. We commend them for that, but only wish that some of the styles had a bit more flair and flattered the larger lady. Sizes 8–22.

Faith
This shoe shop is all about fashion and affordability – lots of party styles and plenty of bright and beautiful shoes. Mostly aimed at the younger shopper. Sizes 3–8.

French Connection
Stylish store and lovely helpful staff. Good for dresses and shirts, great catalogue and online shop. Usually has good linen clothing for summer and plenty of smart, wearable jackets and coats, especially in winter. Colours are well chosen and clothes are made to last. Also has stylish swimwear. Sizes 6–16.

Gap
Excellent range of good quality clothing, with a great selection of jeans in cuts and styles to suit all figures. Always a good selection of wearable summer dresses and shirts at excellent prices. Clothing built to last with a stylish range of accessories to match. Former Chloé designer Phoebe Philo has designed some items. Sizes 4–18.

Hobbs
Smart 'mother of the bride' style clothing, plus a good range of practical, well made, if unsurprising, footwear. Makers of our favourite wear-with-everything low-heeled boot. Shoes in sizes 3–9. Clothing sizes 8–16.

H&M
Fashionable up-to-date styles at excellent prices, including t-shirts from £2.99. Exciting designer collections are regularly launched – previous special collections have been produced by Victor & Rolf, Madonna and Stella McCartney. Sizes 8–16. They also have an excellent Big is Beautiful range in sizes 16–30.

Jaeger
Traditionally a favourite of older professionals and 'Country Life' readers, this shop has attempted to capture the hearts and imaginations of a younger, hipper customer over the past few years. The jury is still out on this store, but there are invariably a number of excellent items on the rails. Sizes 6–18.

Jigsaw
One of the best stores on the high street. Smart formal and work wear alongside fashionable relaxed styles. Good colour palette and clothes are made to last. Look for lovely soft winter coats, pretty dresses, great shirts, excellent knitwear, stylish shoes and boots, brilliant lingerie and loungewear and the best bags ever. Not cheap but wonderful value and they have taken on a new designer so look out for a more directional collection shortly. Sizes 8–16.

Jones
Well made shoes in both classic and fashion styles. Great service, good prices. Sizes 3–8.

Karen Millen
Smart store, good for evening wear and sexy tailored looks. Clothes here are constricting – they're cut small and there are lots of belts, buttons and complicated accessories. Great for figure conscious, showy types – a poorer girl's Versace? Sizes 8–14.

Kurt Geiger
Fantastic shoe shop with all the best high-fashion styles. Designers Marc Jacobs and Chloé stocked in many branches. Also excellent own brand designs. Sizes 3–8.

Lee
Excellent jeans, great fit in all styles. Also good shirts and jackets. Waist sizes 25–32.

Levi's
Founded in 1853, this classic jeans company has come along way since the ubiquitous 501 style that dominated the 1980s. Sells denims made to fit women well. Waist sizes 25–32.

LK Bennett
Brightly coloured shoes with very feminine styling. Lots of satins and evening styles, and good boots in winter. We have yet to see a move forward in their clothing range. Shoe sizes 3–8.

Mango
Spanish chain store with mass-produced, high-fashion items at great prices. T-shirts start at £2.99. There are long queues for the changing rooms on Saturdays and not too much in the way of assistance, especially when busy. Exciting collections are regularly launched by designers such as Milla Jovovich and Victor & Rolf. Mango also do amazing accessories. Sizes 6–14.

Marks & Spencer
Brilliant underwear and hosiery, and good place to find the perfect slip for under that slightly transparent dress. Decent bags and accessories, especially leather goods. Great cashmere, swimwear and sleepwear. Still some frumpy clothes but with some top quality buys mixed in, so a careful look can be really worthwhile. Sizes 8–22. Limited Collection 8–18. Plus 20–28. Lingerie in sizes 32A–38D, with ranges for larger women up to G cup.

Miss Selfridge
Funky, fun and frivolous fashions. Lots of fantastic styles, most of which are designed to show a lot of skin. Miss Selfridge are now competing again in the fashion arena with Topshop. Sizes 6–14.

Miss Sixty
Very popular among the twenty-something crowd. Revealing styles for great bodies. Sizes 8–14.

Monsoon
All things bright and beautiful in this popular high street shop, which has its own successful accessories outlet – Accessorize. Wonderful cosy knitwear in winter, brilliant evening wear, and lots of full-length styles for formal occasions. Sizes 8–22.

New Look
Inexpensive, flirty party clothes for the very young. Also stocks lingerie, sleepwear and lots of bright accessories. Look out for celebrity collections. Sizes 8–18 and Plus Size range 16–28.

Next
This store is a lot more stylish than it used to be. Emphasis is still on the practical, but the clothes are well made and inexpensive. Good work clothing, plenty of middle-management suits and great for basics like raincoats. For a better fit, go down a size when choosing jackets. Sizes 6–22.

Nine West
Great high street shoe shop with very affordable and well made stock. Not high fashion, but you are bound to find a good pair of shoes here. Sizes 3–8.

Oasis
Very stylish high street store with good quality, up-to-the-minute styles, excellent bags and cute shirts. Very good for well cut coats and jackets, lingerie and comfy sleepwear. Also good beachwear in summer and great jewellery. Sizes 8–16.

Office
Wonderful shoe shop with all the latest styles in footwear at affordable prices. Sizes 3–8.

Pepe
A hidden gem. Lovely shirts and dresses at excellent prices. Sizes 8–14.

Primark
It's possible to get a whole new outfit for £10 in Primark. Long queues for changing rooms and tills, so shopping here is not fun but good for throw-away fashions, £5 bikinis and deliberately tacky underwear. Be prepared for a bun fight. Sizes 8–18.

Principles
Well-stocked high street shop with fab dresses and plenty of different ranges to choose from in sizes 6–18. There is an excellent Petite range for ladies under 5' 3''. Plenty of help with fitting and sizing. Sizes 8–20.

Reiss
Good trousers, smart coats and bags, brilliant shift dresses. Very stylish, eye-catching clothing in excellent colours and fabrics. Prada for the high street with a great mix of quality and high style. Sizes 8–14.

High Street Stores

River Island
Another high street great and very popular with teenagers. Hip, a little bit WAG in style but some excellent buys. Sizes 8–14.

Russell & Bromley
Well-styled, high-quality shoes and the best range of boots on the high street every season. Beautiful but pricy sandals and an attractive range of court shoes. Prices only a little less than Prada. Sizes 3–8.

Schuh
Fantastic high street shoe shop with a wide range of styles to suit everyone from the very young and trendy to the more 'mature' shopper. Sizes 3–8. Up to 9 in some stores.

Ted Baker
Excellent women's wear collection. They get things just right – not frumpy, nor too fashionable. Good bags as well. Sizes 8–14.

T K Maxx
This is the high street lucky dip! Among the racks and racks of designer rejects there may just be that perfect purchase in your size. You need to be a patient, diligent shopper – definitely not for the faint hearted. Sizes depend on label but plenty of choice for all.

Topshop
High fashion styles at very affordable prices. Larger stores can be overwhelming, especially at weekends when Topshop traditionally becomes the destination of choice for every teenager in town. Great shoes and accessories. The store regularly launches designer ranges such as the much promoted Kate Moss collection. Sizes 6–16.

Urban Outfitters
Fun fashion store from the US – a little grungy/punky but well worth checking out. Sells Cheap Monday skinny jeans, cool smock dresses, hip labels and also plenty of cute accessories. The Kensington branch in London has a more expensive designer room upstairs, featuring diffusion lines from Sonia Rykiel and Chloé – you could end up spending a fortune! Sizes 8–16 but varies as so many different ranges are stocked.

Wallis
A major revamp of designs has exorcised granny ghosts from Wallis. Instead of dull, outdated styles you will now find nice evening wear alongside basics such as simple trousers, jackets and smart blouses. Every season they produce some excellent fashion items and they have a great eye for colour and styles that work for all kinds of shapes. Great for larger sizes and a good Petite range too. Sizes 8–20.

Warehouse
Eye-catching dresses and accessories and some attractive but relaxed styles. A good place to shop for clothing for holidays and casual evenings out. Sizes 6–16.

Whistles
Lovely dresses, smart coats and pretty accessories. Lots of florals, plenty of ribbons and frills in this very feminine store. Great shoes and bags as well. Sizes 8–16.

Zara
The Spanish chain that changed the face of the European high street. High-fashion styles reproduced at lightning speed and retailed at very affordable prices. Stocks good basics and office wear as well as fab dresses and super-hip catwalk styles. Great for essential winter coats and skirts, trousers and dresses in the right shapes for our rules. Sizes 6–18.

Internet shopping

www.accessoriesonline.co.uk
Loads of fabulous accessories from designers such as Butler & Wilson, Les Nereides and more.

www.allalts.co.uk
It may sound mad to send your clothes away for alterations, but this is a rather clever idea. You pin the item that needs altering, pop it in the post and seven days later you get it back. Great for people who don't have time to go to the local dry cleaners – but you do need to get to the post office.

www.babyceylon.com
A piece of Portobello market at your fingertips – beautiful clothes from this iconic little boutique.

www.belindarobertson.com
Beautiful cashmere jumpers delivered to your door.

www.blossommotherandchild.com
Upmarket maternity wear. It may be on the expensive side, but check this site out if you want to maintain a bit of glamour during your pregnancy.

www.brownsfashion.com
Perfect for the serious shopa-holic, this site offers the best labels on earth! Check out Browns Focus for the more cutting-edge designers. On this site you can find clothes by Fendi, Dosa, Balenciaga, Acne Jeans and Vanessa Bruno.

www.bunnyhug.co.uk
Gorgeous site with tons of young hip labels, from Cheap Monday jeans, Ella Moss and Splendid, to Tom Ford sunglasses.

www.cinnamonfashion.co.uk
Brilliant site which caters for sizes 16–34. You do need to have a good surf around, however, as there are some dodgy items amid it all.

www.cocoribbon.com
Delicious boudoir boutique with the most beautiful bits and bobs, including clothes, accessories and gifts. Very tempting to have a serious shopping spree. Sass & Bide, Damaris and Manoush.

www.figleaves.com
There is so much choice and they go up to large bra sizes such as 48–56 FF. You can also buy maternity bras on this site. Delivery is quick.

www.frillybylily.co.uk
If you are looking for quirky jewellery this site is what you need – gorgeous bracelets and necklaces. Check out the bits and bobs section, too.

www.kabiri.co.uk
The most amazing jewellery shop. Designers include Alexis Bittar, Me & Ro, Phillip Crangi, Tom Binns and Carolina Bucci.

www.lastarstyle.com
Genius site for those of you who are obsessed with what celebs are wearing… get the latest trends on here.

www.littlewoods.com
Great clothes online for all body shapes at high street prices – with free expert style advice from us! Plus it's the only place you can get exclusive trinny&susannah clothing.

www.matchesfashion.com
Amazing designer range available online. Be ready to do some serious credit card damage. Designers include Jovovich-Hawk, Lanvin, Temperley, Luella, Velvet… the list goes on and on.

www.my-wardrobe.com
Loads of designer labels which you can order online, such as Antik Batik, C & C California, Juicy Couture, Milla, Tom Ford sunglasses to name but a few.

www.net-a-porter.com
The mother of all fashion sites. All the latest designer collections at your fingertips, including Derek Lam, Zac Posen, Proenza Schouler, Chloé, Celine, Issa and loads more.

www.pollyanna.com
Visionary fashion store, with labels such as Issey Miyake, Jil Sander and many more.

www.satineboutique.com
Fabulous online shop selling ranges direct from LA. So many mouth-watering labels – check out the 'items we idolize' section and be inspired. Designers include Cheap Monday, Webster, Wilson, Clu and Sass & Bide.

www.shoestudio.com
All the high street shoes you need in one place, including Pied à Terre, Bertie and Nine West.

www.spirito.co.uk
Chic and smart clothing sized from 14–30. So many gorgeous styles, it's hard to choose.

www.topshop.co.uk
The ultimate site for any self-respecting fashion lover.

www.urbanoutfitters.co.uk
The coolest shop on the high street. If you're looking for quirky fashion this is the ideal site. Designers include Alice McCall, Hussein Chalayan, Sara Berman and Cacharel.

www.uggstore.com.au
Original Ugg boots from Australia.

www.vivaladiva.com
Shoe heaven, from designer to high street. They also have shoes for wide feet. Designers include Converse, Havainas, Luc Berjen, Terry de Havilland and Georgina Goodman.

www.yoox.com
This site offers every label under the sun and is bursting with end of season stock at fantastic prices. Designers include Missoni, Dosa, Prada, Costume National and Marni.

Aberdeen

HIGH STREET

Dorothy Perkins
115 The Trinity Centre,
Aberdeen AB11. 01224 578536

French Connection
Unit 2–3 The Academy Shopping
Centre, Belmont St, Aberdeen
AB10. 01224 627411

Gap
7–21A St Nicholas Street,
Aberdeen AB10. 01224 635405

H&M
57–63 Union Street, Aberdeen
AB11. 020 8382 3253

Miss Selfridge
Unit E9 St Nicholas Centre,
Aberdeen AB10. 01224 646747

Monsoon
5 & 33 Bon Accord Centre, George
Street, Aberdeen AB25.
01224 649146

Oasis
Unit 17–18 Bon Accord Centre,
George Street, Aberdeen AB25.
01224 636727

Primark
143–153 Union Street, Aberdeen
AB11. 01224 213828

River Island
1 St Nicholas Centre, Aberdeen
AB10. 01224 647253

Topshop
73–77 Union Street, Aberdeen
AB11. 01224 590710

BOUTIQUES, DESIGNERS AND INDEPENDENT STORES

AB10
The Academy Centre, Belmont
Street, Aberdeen AB10.
01224 637965
Youthful fashions from D&G, Ted
Baker and Miss Sixty, alongside
a great selection of footwear and
accessories.

Kafka
5 Alford Place, Aberdeen AB10.
01224 626 002
We've never thought of clothes
shopping as a subject worthy of
the Czech novelist but maybe they
have a point... Kafka stocks
Armani, Burberry, Prada, Prada
Sport, Paul Smith, Maxmara, 7
For All Mankind, Mulberry, Chloé.

Bellino
17 Thistle Street, Aberdeen AB10.
01224 648130
A varied, range of shoes, boots
and handbags.

Zoomp
Jopps Lane, Aberdeen AB25.
01224 642152
From everyday casual to Jimmy
Choo and Matthew Williamson.
You'll find everything you need for
those Carrie Bradshaw moments
in Zoomp.

DEPARTMENT STORES

John Lewis
George Street, Aberdeen AB25.
01224 625000
Sensible clothing from Hobbs,
Warehouse, Coast, Principles,
Esprit and Phase Eight. Shoes by
Kurt Geiger, and lingerie by Calvin
Klein.

Debenhams
Trinity Centre, 155 Union Street,
Aberdeen AB11. 0844 5 616161
Includes branches of Topshop and
Dorothy Perkins.

VINTAGE

The Closet
31 Jopps Lane, Aberdeen AB25.
01224 625450
Clothes from the 1950s–1980s,
but occasionally older items are
in stock.

SALONS, SPAS AND BEAUTY STORES

James Dun's House
Aveda Lifestyle Salon, 61
Schoolhill, Aberdeen, AB15.
01224 648480
Smart salon offering Aveda
treatments.

Bath and Bristol

HIGH STREET

French Connection
9 New Broadmead, Union Street,
Bristol BS1. 0117 926 8108

H&M
Odeon Buildings, Union Street,
Broadmead, Bristol BS1.
0117 945 1870

Jigsaw
8 New Bond Street, Bath BA1.
01225 461613

Karen Millen
68 Queens Road, Bristol BS8.
0117 926 4085

Miss Selfridge
81 Broadmead, Bristol BS1.
0117 930 4402

Monsoon
7 New Broadmead, Union Street,
Bristol BS1. 0117 929 0870

Oasis
20 Cheap Street, Bath BA1.
01225 442922

Office
6 New Broadmead, Union Street,
Bristol BS1. 0117 929 4434

Primark
82–92 The Horsefair, Bristol BS1.
0117 927 7391

River Island
7–8 Stall Street, Bath BA1.
01225 466205

BOUTIQUES, DESIGNERS AND INDEPENDENT STORES

Allure
17 Regent Street, Bristol BS8.
0117 974 3882
Beautiful clothes from Antik Batik,
Rutzou, Poleci, Libelula, Bruuns
Bazaar, By Malene Birger, Luc
Bergen and more.

Annabel Harrison/AH Moda
14–15 Shires Yard, Milsom Street,
Bath BA1. 01225 447598
Collections from Nicole Farhi,
Wheels & DollBaby, Da Nang,
Citizens of Humanity, Rock &
Republic, and Moschino.

Duo
33 Milsom Street, Bath BA1.
01225 460745
The world's leading specialist in
calf-fitting boots, including a
stunning 'off the shelf' range in 27
designs and a variety of colours
and materials.

Prey
3 York Buildings, Bath BA1.
01225 329933
Alana Hill, Orla Kiely, Tara Jarman,
Betty Jackson, Somi, Tocca,
Transit. Also perfumes by Creed
and Annick Goutal.

John Anthony
108 Broadmead, Bristol BS1.
0117 922 0799
Designer boutique featuring shoes,
clothing and accessories from
Roberto Cavalli, Dolce & Gabbana,
Vivienne Westwood, Moschino,
DSquared, Ralph Lauren, 7 For All
Mankind. There is an in-house
tailoring service so you can get a
perfect fit.

Oyster:Me
37 Princess Victoria Street, Bristol
BS8. 0117 923 9431
Lingerie by Mimi Holiday, Bas Bleu,
Eberjey and Pistol Panties as well
as an excellent range of equally
appealing swimwear.

18 18
The Mall, Clifton, Bristol BS8.
0117 974 5332
Lovely boutique stocking Essential,
Stella Forest, Twinset and others,
with shoes from French Sole and
beautiful bags from Angel.

DEPARTMENT STORES

House of Fraser
The Horsefair, Broadmead, Bristol,
BS1. 0117 944 5566

Jollys Department Store
7–14 Milsom Street, Bath BA1.
01225 462811

VINTAGE

Vintage to Vogue
28 Milsom Street, Bath BA1.
01225 337323
Beautiful vintage clothing from
Victorian era to 1950s.
Open Tues–Sat, 11–5pm.

Jack & Danny's
3 London Street, Bath BA1.
01225 469972
Racks of funky vintage clothing and
accessories especially from the 60s
and 70s are packed into this
fantastic store, which also sells
vintage musical instruments

Fountain Antiques Centre
3 Fountain Buildings, Lansdown
Road, Bath BA1. 01225 428731
Two floors of antiques including
traders in jewellery, clothing, bags
and fabrics.
Open Mon–Sat, 9–5pm

Clifton Hill Antiques
5 Lower Clifton Hill, Bristol BS8.
0117 929 0644
Interesting and unique selection of
vintage clothing from all eras.

SALONS, SPAS AND BEAUTY STORES

Thermae Bath Spa
The Hetling Pump Room, Hot Bath
St, Bath BA1. 01225 331234.
www.thermaebathspa.com
Two-hour spa sessions in thermal
mineral waters from £20, as well a
range of tempting spa packages.
The spa consists of the Cross
Baths, an outdoor spa built on the
original Celtic and Roman spa site
and the New Royal Bath, a luxurious new spa near the original site.

The Relaxation Centre
9 All Saints Road, Clifton, Bristol
BS8. 0117 970 6616
A unique environment dedicated to
relaxation: saunas, steam room,
hot tub, spa, floatation room,
relaxation lounge, meditation room,
massage and much more.
Everything you need to soothe
away stress, worries, aches and
pains.

The Royal Crescent Hotel & Bath House Spa
16 Royal Crescent, Bath BA1.
01225 823333
Half-day retreats available at this
exclusive hotel on the famous
Royal Crescent. Have a delicious
lunch followed by treatments at the
Bath House spa set in the hotel
grounds.

Belfast

HIGH STREET

French Connection
26–28 Corn Market, Belfast BT1.
02890 246799

Kookai
49 Royal Avenue, Belfast BT1.
02890 320314

Monsoon
1–9 Donegal Place, Belfast BT1.
02890 237841

Oasis
25–27 Donegal Place, Belfast BT1.
02890 240105

Primark
Bank Buildings, Belfast BT1.
02890 242288

The Original Levi's Store
12 Donegal Place, Belfast BT1.
02890 244633

Topshop
51 Donegal Place, Belfast BT1.
02890 323221

Wallis
18-22 Castle Place, Belfast BT1.
02890 326836

Warehouse
Unit 2, Castle Court Shopping
Centre, Belfast BT1. 02890 439606

Zara
3 Donegal Place, Belfast BT1.
02890 445330

BOUTIQUES, DESIGNERS AND INDEPENDENT STORES

BT9/Paul Costello
45 Bradbury Place, Belfast BT7.
02890 239496
Orla Kiely, James Jeans, 7 For All
Mankind, Sabatini.

Bureau Women Ltd
1–2 Wellington Street, Belfast BT1.
02890 311110
Beautiful clothes from Paul Smith,
Miu Miu, Dries van Noten, Camper
and Calvin Klein.

Harper Lesley Plaza
406 Lisbon Road, Belfast BT9.
02890 681556
Celine, Chloé, Burberry, 120%
Linen, Mulberry and Armani.

Honey
627 Lisburn Road, Belfast BT9.
02890 667466
If the 'Sex and the City' girls lived in
Belfast, this is where they'd shop.
Fab designer lingerie, shoes and
accessories.

Rojo
613 Lisburn Road, Belfast BT9.
02890 666998
Shoes by Prada, Pollini, Gucci,
Chanel, DKNY, Stuart Weitzman
and Kenzo.

The Glasshouse
16–22 Bedford House, Bedford
Street, Belfast BT2. 02890 312964
Clothing from Nicole Farhi, Paul
Smith, Joseph and Whistles.

DEPARTMENT STORES

Debenhams
Unit 34, Castle Court, Royal
Avenue, Belfast BT1.
0844 5 616161
Stocks Red Herring, Nike,
Gorgeous, Principles and the
Debenhams Collection. Also an
excellent selection of lingerie and
a good beauty hall.

VINTAGE

Rusty Zip
28 Botanic Avenue, Belfast BT7.
02890 249700
Second-hand shop with amazing
designer bargains to be found.

Liberty Blue
9 Lombard Street, Belfast BT1.
02890 437745
Quirky and original would sum up
this gem of a shop.

SALONS, SPAS AND BEAUTY STORES

Aura Day Spa
615 Lisburn Road, Belfast BT9.
02890 666277
A range of aromatherapy and
massage treatments available along
with infra-red sauna and dry
floatation therapy. Also facials using
Guinot products.

Culloden Estate and Spa
Bangor Road, Holywood, Belfast
BT18. 02890 421066
Luxury treatments in five-star
surroundings.

Birmingham

HIGH STREET

French Connection
The Bullring Shopping Centre,
Birmingham B5. 0121 633 9304

H&M
76–78 Corporation Street,
Birmingham B2. 0121 232 8090

Jigsaw
Caxton Gate, 8 Cannon Street,
Birmingham B2. 0121 633 9475

Mango
Bullring, Level 2, Birmingham B5.
0121 643 6019

New Look
51 The Pallasades, Birmingham
B2. 0121 632 5589

Oasis
Unit 1, 125-126, New Street,
Birmingham B2. 0121 643 2770

Reiss
Upper Mall East, Bullring,
Birmingham B5. 0121 616 1191

Topshop
Unit 2b, Bullring, Birmingham B2.
0121 643 0348

Urban Outfitters
Caxton Gate, 5 Corporation Street,
Birmingham B2. 0121 633 2920

Zara
148 New Street, Birmingham B2.
0121 616 0600

BOUTIQUES, DESIGNERS AND INDEPENDENT STORES

Daniel Footwear
Wharfside Street, The Mailbox,
Birmingham B1. 0121 632 1421
Glamorous shoes from Dior,
Missoni, Gina, and Roberto Cavalli.

Flannels
14 Lower Temple Street,
Birmingham B2. 0121 633 0529
Range includes Dolce & Gabbana,
Gucci, Prada, Issa, Diane von
Furstenberg, Matthew Williamson,
Armani and Joseph.

Louis Vuitton
71 Temple Row, Birmingham B2.
0121 616 2044
No clothing in this store but a
range of beautifully crafted bags,
shoes, wallets and watches.

Onu
3 Stephenson Street, Birmingham
B2. 0121 643 3434
Stocks Versace, Armani and Evisu
to name but a few.

Ronit Zilkha
21 Royal Arch Apartments,
Birmingham B1. 0121 643 2826
Stylish and sweet dresses.

DEPARTMENT STORES

Selfridges
Upper Mall East, Bullring,
Birmingham B5. 0870 837 7377
Worth a visit to see the landmark
building by Future Systems.
Includes branches of Miss Sixty,
LK Bennett, Kurt Geiger and Agent
Provocateur. Also has designer
ranges from Alaia, Alexander
McQueen, Burberry Prorsum,
Eres, Issa, Antik Batik, Gina,
Prada, Ann Demeulemeester,
Miu Miu and many more.

Harvey Nichols
31 Wharfside Street, Birmingham
B1. 0121 616 6000
Collections include Missoni,
L.A.M.B, McQ, Dolce & Gabbana,
Citizens of Humanity, 18th
Amendment, Gucci and Versace.

VINTAGE/MARKETS

The Saturday Flea
The Custard Factory, Gibbs
Square, Birmingham B9.
0121 224 7777
Vintage market open from 10–5pm
on Saturdays. Stalls sell bags,
textiles, clothing and jewellery.

Urban Village
86 Hurst Street, Birmingham B5.
0121 622 5351
Clothing from 1950s–1980s.

Yoyo
7 Ethel Street Birmingham B2.
0121 633 3073
Clothing from 1950s–1980s.

Retro Bizarre
25 St Mary's Row, Moseley,
Birmingham B13. 0121 442 6389
Occasional Edwardian pieces,
some 1920s but mostly clothes
from 1930s–1980s.

SALONS, SPAS AND BEAUTY STORES

Le Petit Spa at Malmaison Hotel
The Mailbox, 1 Wharfside,
Birmingham B1. 0121 246 5008
Day packages, massage and
Elemis Advanced Performance
Facials at the city's sexiest spa.

Brighton

HIGH STREET

All Saints
35 Duke Street, Brighton BN1.
01273 710107

French Connection
55 East Street, Brighton BN1.
01273 727117

Jigsaw
53–54 East Street, Brighton BN1.
01273 206988

Kurt Geiger
1 North Street, Brighton BN4.
01273 749727

LK Bennett
38–39 East Street, Brighton BN1.
01273 722 988

Mango
4 North Street, Brighton BN1.
01273 203355

Primark
188–191 Western Road, Brighton
BN1. 01273 205211

Topshop
95-99 Churchill Square, Brighton
BT1. 01273 724696

Warehouse
Churchill Square Shopping Centre,
Brighton BN1. 01273 204815

Zara
Churchill Square Shopping Centre,
Brighton BN1. 01273 74018

BOUTIQUES, DESIGNERS AND INDEPENDENT STORES

Badger Clothing
26 Bond Street, Brighton BN1.
01273 722245
Casual clothing from Evisu, Diesel,
Birkenstock and others.

Brief Encounter
13 Brighton Square, Brighton BN1.
01273 208404
Chantelle, Cotton Club, La Perla
and an irresistible selection of
lingerie.

Profile
4 Duke's Lane, Brighton BN1.
01273 733561
Stocks Armani, Versace and Ralph
Lauren.

Simultane
52 Ship Street Brighton BN1.
01273 777535
Designer Sarah Arnett shows a
range of ready-to-wear dresses
alongside a 'made to order'
portfolio for special occasions.
This beautiful shop also stocks
designs from Madeleine Press, Issa
and Marilyn Moore, and knitwear
from Marcus Lupfer.

DEPARTMENT STORES

Debenhams
95-99 Churchill Square, Brighton
BN1. 0870 600 3333
Alongside the Debenhams' own
range of fashions, this shop has
concessions of Kaliko, Oasis,
Wallis, Principles and La Senza.

VINTAGE

30a Upper St James Street,
Brighton BN2. 01273 681384
Women's wear from the 1920s
onwards with occasional earlier
pieces. Open Thurs–Sat, 11–5.30.

Harlequin Vintage
31 Sydney Street, Brighton BN1.
01273 675222
Clothing from 1940s onwards.

Rokit
23 Kensington Gardens, Brighton
BN1. 01273 672053
www.rokit.co.uk
Clothing from the 1960s, 70s, 80s
and 90s.

StarFish
25 Gardener Street, Brighton BN1.
01273 680868
Collection of women's clothing,
bags and shoes from all eras

Yellow Submarine
12 Kensington Gardens, Brighton
BN1. 01273 626435
Wide range of inexpensive, original
clothing from all eras, particularly
the 1970s.

To Be Worn Again
51 Providence Place, Brighton
BN1. 01273 624500
Clothing from 1960s, 70s and 80s.

SALONS, SPAS AND BEAUTY STORES

Lansdowne Place Hotel Spa
Lansdowne Place, Brighton BN3.
01273 732839
Body treatments from detoxifying
algae wrap to full aromatherapy
body massage. There are 8 treatment rooms in this newly built spa,
including 2 dual-treatment rooms
so you can enjoy an Espa treatment with a friend – although why
you would want to we don't know.

L'Occitane
23a East St, Brighton BN1.
01273 719171
Divine bubble baths and body
lotions from Provence.

Pecksniffs
45–46 Meeting House Lane,
Brighton BN1. 01273 723292
Makers of bespoke floral and
essential oil scents and bath
products, all of which are beautifully
packaged.

The Lanes Health & Beauty Clinic
50–52 Market Street, Brighton
BN1. 01273 725572
Range of hair, face and body treatments including oxygen facials, and
beach body salt scrubs using the
Thalgo range.

Cambridge

HIGH STREET

Dorothy Perkins
8 Grafton Centre, Cambridge CB1.
01223 323674

French Connection
16 Market Hill, Cambridge CB2.
01223 311966

Jigsaw
22 Market Street, Cambridge CB2.
01223 312955

Karen Millen
10 Market Street, Cambridge CB2.
01223 304502

Miss Selfridge
Unit 14–15 Lion Yard Centre,
Cambridge CB2.
01223 369289

Oasis
5 Market Hill, Cambridge CB2.
01223 300641

Reiss
26 Trinity Street, Cambridge CB2.
01223 308733

Topshop
31 Petty Cury, Cambridge CB2.
01223 367499

Wallis
Unit 27a, Grafton Centre,
Cambridge CB1. 01223 461719

Warehouse
14 Grafton Centre, Cambridge
CB1. 01223 352559

BOUTIQUES, DESIGNERS AND INDEPENDENT STORES

Boudoir Femme
18 King Street, Cambridge CB1.
01223 323000
Exclusive collection of luxury
designer and vintage clothing,
accessories and other bits and
bobs.

Bowns
25 Magdalene Street, Cambridge
CB3. 01223 302000
Women's wear, including John
Rocha, Paul & Joe, Boyd, Vivienne
Westwood, Ultra Ozbek.

Bravissimo
17 Sussex Street, Cambridge CB1.
01223 356088
Great bras and swimsuits for big
boobs.

Cuckoo
Burwash Manor Barns, Barton,
Cambridge CB3. 01223 262123
Eclectic selection of vintage
clothes, accessories and jewellery.

Ghost
3 Green Street, Cambridge CB2.
01223 354436
Floaty dresses in every colour.

Giulio Woman
5–7 Sussex Street, Cambridge
CB1. 01223 316166
Designer clothes by Armani, Gucci,
Prada, Burberry, Valentino, Versace,
Pringle.

Le Reve
6 Benet Street, Cambridge CB2.
01223 328111
Designer lingerie, from ranges such
as La Perla and Rigby & Peller.

Troon
16 Kings Parade, Cambridge CB2.
01223 360274
Designer boutique stocking Betty
Jackson, Gharani Strok, Georgina
von Etzdorf, Margaret Howell, Jean
Muir and more.

DEPARTMENT STORES

Debenhams
36–40 Grafton Centre, Cambridge
CB1. 0844 5 616161
Stocks Coast, Principles, Topshop,
Warehouse, Jaques Vert as well as
Debenham's own range.

VINTAGE

Vera Vintage Clothing
The Hive, 3 Dales Brewery,
Cambridge CB1. 01223 300269
www.veravintageclothing.co.uk
Specialises in evening and special
occasion wear from the 1920s–
1950s.

SALONS, SPAS AND BEAUTY STORES

Molton Brown
5 Rose Crescent, Cambridge CB2.
01223 353954
Cosmetics & beauty products,
facials and makeovers, using their
own excellent products.

Neal's Yard Remedies
1 Rose Crescent, Cambridge CB2.
01223 321074
Organic beauty products, treatments and herbal remedies.

S'Amuser
5 Benet Street, Cambridge CB2.
01223 308942
Bespoke perfumery: individual
scents are mixed and made to
order from a wide range of natural
oils and extracts.

The Reflections Spa
The Cambridge Belfry, Cambourne,
Cambridge CB3. 01954 714620
Luxury treatments using the Espa
range of products.

Cardiff

HIGH STREET

Dorothy Perkins
17 Queen Street, Cardiff CF10.
02920 387357

Faith
Unit 15 Queens Arcade, Queen
Street, Cardiff CF1. 02920 232045

Gap
10–11 Queens Arcade, Queen
Street, Cardiff CF10.
02920 340464

H&M
Capitol Shopping Centre, Queen
Street, Cardiff CF10.
02920 727950

Karen Millen
Unit 6, Capitol Shopping Centre,
Queen Street, Cardiff CF10.
02920 666515

Next
82–88 Queen Street, Cardiff CF10.
0870 386 5233

Oasis
46–50 St David's Way, Cardiff
CF10. 02920 220875

River Island
Unit 3, The Andrews Building,
Queen Street, Cardiff CF10.
02920 229051

Topshop
46–50 St David's Way, Cardiff
CF10. 02920 381540

Zara
The Andrews Building, Queen
Street, Cardiff CF10.
02920 537600

BOUTIQUES, DESIGNERS AND INDEPENDENT STORES

Chiesa
186–188 Kings Road, Cardiff CF11.
02920 233559
Charlotte Church's mother brings
Italian styling to Cardiff. The shop
has designs from Grace, Monica
Ricci, Adini and Billy Bag.

Poppers
75 Pontcanna Street, Cardiff CF11.
02920 342568
Hip boutique stocking Gerard
Darel, Indies and Ischiko.

Prey
6–8 Morgan Arcade, Cardiff CF10.
02920 233293
Stocks Megan Park, Transit, Alana
Hill, Rutzou, Tocca, Saltwater,
Tara Jarmon, Karen Cole. Also a
beautiful jewellery collection and
perfumes by Creed.

Staging Seduction
The Aspect, 140 Queen Street,
Cardiff CF10. 02920 224619
A paradise of renowned brands
such as Dolce & Gabbana, Hugo
Boss, Diesel, Hardy Amies, Gucci,
Prada, Armani, Ralph Lauren and
Gina.

DEPARTMENT STORES

House of Fraser
14 St Mary Street, Cardiff CF10.
02920 341112
Large branch that stocks D&G,
Pink Soda, Nougat, Whistles,
Ghost, Therapy, Kurt Geiger and
Nine West. Good beauty hall on the
ground floor.

VINTAGE AND MARKETS

Drop Dead Budgie
10–12 Royal Arcade, The Hayes,
Cardiff CF10. 02920 398891
Unique clothing and accessories
shop, which emphasises the
environmental benefits of recycling
clothing

Hobos
26 High Street Arcade, Cardiff
CF10. 02920 341188
Fun fashions from the 1950s, 60s
and 70s.

Retro – Centric
Unit 2, Newport Arcade, High
Street, Newport NP2.
01633 270899
Eclectic selection of vintage
clothing and accessories

Tail & The Unexpected
10 Victoria Road, Penarth, Vale,
Glamorgan CF64. 02920 704499
This excellent vintage store is part
of the Jacob's Antique Market.

SALONS, SPAS AND BEAUTY STORES

Neal's Yard Remedies
23–25 Morgan Arcade, Cardiff CF1.
02920 235721
Lovely aromatherapy bubble baths
and body lotions, excellent face
creams and skin toners made from
orange flowers and roses.

Spa at St David's Hotel
Havannah Street, Cardiff CF10.
02920 313084
Luxurious day packages available.
Hydrotherapy pools, Thalasso
facials and body wraps – pure
relaxation in five-star surroundings.

Dublin

HIGH STREET

French Connection
Powerscourt Centre, Clarendon
Street, Dublin. 01 670 8199

H&M
Blanchardstown Shopping Centre,
Navan Road, Dublin. 01 299 1517

Jigsaw
42 Grafton Street, Dublin.
01 671 3546

Karen Millen
Powerscourt Centre, Clarendon
Street, Dublin. 01 670 0282

Reiss
1 North Street, St Stephen's Green,
Dublin. 01 671 2588

Topshop
Blanchardstown Shopping Centre,
Navan Road, Dublin. 01 822 1874

Urban Outfitters
4 Cecilia Street, Dublin.
01 670 6202

Warehouse
37 Grafton Street, Dublin.
01 677 7719

Whistles
18 Balfe Street, Dublin.
01 670 8199

Zara
Blanchardstown Shopping Centre,
Navan Road, Dublin. 01 817 9000

BOUTIQUES, DESIGNERS AND INDEPENDENT STORES

BT2
28–29 Grafton Street, Dublin.
01 605 6666
Younger sister of Brown Thomas,
with less expensive, hip designs
aimed at younger customers. Acne
Jeans, Custo, Betsey Johnson.

CoCo Woman
Powerscourt Centre, Clarendon
Street, Dublin. 01 707 9960
Feminine designs with the focus on
colour and fit. Designers stocked
include Lungren and Pocket Venus.

Genius
Powerscourt Centre, Clarendon
Street, Dublin. 01 679 7851
Featuring top high street ranges,
including Diesel, Gas, Miss Sixty,
Melting Pot and Energie.

Kilkenny
5/6 Nassau Street, Dublin.
01 677 7066
Design store featuring the best of
Irish talent in home wear, jewellery
and fashion. The shop has its own
range of clothing called the Art of
Dressing and features collections
from Orla Kiely, Kate Cooper and
Aileen Bodkin.

DEPARTMENT STORES

Brown Thomas
Grafton Street, Dublin.
01 605 6666
A wonderful department store with
the emphasis on luxury. Designs
from Chanel, Christian Dior, Chloé,
Amanda Wakeley, Biba, Burberry
Prorsum, Armani, DSquared,
Jimmy Choo, and all the big name
fashion houses. Younger, hipper
and less expensive designs are
stocked at BT2 across the road.

Harvey Nichols
Dundrum Town Centre, Sandyford
Road, Dublin. 01 291 0488
Three floors of fashion and beauty
with collections from Armani
Collezioni, DSquared, Megan Park,
Nina Ricci, Matthew Williamson,
Just Cavalli, Andrew GN, 3.1 Phillip
Lim, Galliano, Pucci and Vera Wang
Lavender. There is also a restaurant
and scrumptious food hall.

VINTAGE

A Store Is Born
34 Clarendon Street, Dublin.
01 679 5866
Antique clothing market renowned
for evening wear.

Big Whiskey
Market Arcade, Dublin.
01 679 9299
Jammed with second-hand
clothing.

Flip
4 Upper Fownes Street, Dublin.
01 671 0202
Retro clothing from the 1950s,
60s and 70s.

Jenny Vander
20 Market Arcade, George Street,
Dublin. 01 677 0406
Antique jewellery, ball gowns and
other gems.

SeSi
13 Temple Bar Square, Dublin.
01 679 0523
Vintage shoes, bags and a wide
range of jewellery.

SALONS, SPAS AND BEAUTY STORES

The Day Dream Health Spa
5–7 Terenure Place, Dublin.
01 499 0111
Relax in the Serenity Lounge
and enjoy a range of excellent
treatments using Aveda and
Dermalogica Products.

**The Spa at
The Four Seasons Hotel**
Simonscourt Road, Dublin.
01 665 4000
Hot stone therapies and La Prairie
facials in luxurious surroundings.

Edinburgh

HIGH STREET

Coast
61 George Street, Edinburgh EH2.
0131 226 4995

French Connection
68–70 George Street, Edinburgh
EH2. 0131 220 1276

Jigsaw
49 George Street, Edinburgh EH2.
0131 225 4501

Karen Millen
53 George Street, Edinburgh EH2.
0131 220 1589

Marks & Spencer
54 Princes Street, Edinburgh EH2.
0131 225 2301

Miss Selfridge
13–21 Hanover Street, Edinburgh
EH2. 0131 220 1209

Reiss
24 Multrees Walk, Edinburgh EH1.
0131 557 5008

TK Maxx
Unit 10, Meadowbank Retail Park,
Edinburgh EH7. 0131 661 6611

Whistles
97 George Street, Edinburgh EH2.
0131 226 4398

Zara
104–106 Princes Street, Edinburgh
EH2. 0131 240 3230

BOUTIQUES, DESIGNERS AND INDEPENDENT STORES

Anne Fontaine
4 Multrees Walk, Edinburgh EH1.
0131 558 1284
Classic white shirts.

Boudiche
15 Frederick Street, Edinburgh
EH2. 0131 226 5255
Divine lingerie from some of the
best designers, including Mimi
Holiday, Damaris, Beau Bra and
Chantelle.

Cruise
94 George Street, Edinburgh EH2.
0131 226 3524
Established designer boutique
carrying Marni, Prada, Gucci, Paul
Smith, and Dolce & Gabbana.

Cruise Jeans
14 George Street, Edinburgh EH2.
0131 226 0840
Designer jeans and general cool
stuff.

Godiva
9 West Port, Grassmarket,
Edinburgh EH1. 0131 221 9212
Vintage pieces alongside new
ranges by recent fashion design
graduates, as well as one-off items.

Jane Davidson
52 Thistle Street, Edinburgh EH2.
0131 225 3280
Three floors of desirable shoes and
clothing from fashion greats such
as Jimmy Choo, Diane von
Furstenberg, La Perla and others.

Mulberry
6 Multrees Walk, Edinburgh EH1.
0131 557 5439
This shop stocks only the fantastic
handbags – sadly no clothes.

DEPARTMENT STORES

Harvey Nichols
32–34 St Andrews Square,
Edinburgh EH2. 0131 524 8388
Collections from Cacharel, Cesare
Fabbri, Edun, Gucci, D&G, Chloé,
Donna Karan, Nicole Farhi, Shirin
Guild, Michael Kors, Rock &
Republic, and loads more!

VINTAGE

Armstrongs Vintage Clothing
83 Grassmarket, Edinburgh EH1.
0131 220 5557
Eclectic collection of vintage clothing. Plenty of items pre-1950s.

Armstrongs
64–66 Clerk Street, Edinburgh
EH8. 0131 667 3056
Smaller branch of above store.

Elaine's Vintage Clothing
55 St Stephen Street, Edinburgh
EH3. 0131 225 5783
Specialist in 40s and 50s clothing,

Flip of Hollywood
59–61 South Bridge, Edinburgh
EH1. 0131 556 4966
American retro clothing.

Herman Brown
151 West Port, Edinburgh EH3.
0131 228 2589
Family-run vintage shop with
clothing from 1930s onwards.

SALONS, SPAS AND BEAUTY STORES

Charlie Miller Hair Salon
39 Frederick Street, Edinburgh
EH2. 0131 225 1141
Also at Harvey Nichols 2nd Floor,
0131 524 8356.
Try the Toa head massage – 30
minutes of heaven before you have
your hair beautifully styled.

Jo Malone
93 George Street, Edinburgh EH2.
0131 478 8555
Delicious products and facials.

L'Occitane
18b Frederick Street, Edinburgh
EH2. 0131 226 5350
Gorgeous products at great prices.

Vidal Sassoon Studio
10 The Walk, St Andrews Square,
Edinburgh EH1 0131 558 2849
Fancy a great haircut and blow
dry? This is Britain's original trendy
hairdresser.

Zen Lifestyle
9 Bruntsfield Street, Edinburgh
EH1. 0131 477 3535
Glycolic peels, oxygen facials and
massage using products such as
Aveda and Elemis.

Exeter

HIGH STREET

Dorothy Perkins
12 High Street, Exeter EX4.
01392 439364

Evans
231 High Street, Exeter EX4.
01392 272046

Gap
8–9 High Street, Exeter EX4.
01392 424080

H&M
16–20 High Street, Exeter EX4.
01392 260380

Jones
238 High Street, Exeter EX4.
01392 210355

Marks & Spencer
211–219 High Street, Exeter EX4.
01392 214999

Miss Selfridge
247 High Street, Exeter EX4.
01392 495767

Oasis
35 High Street, Exeter EX4.
01392 459528

Office
240 High Street, Exeter EX4.
01392 495615

Topshop
228 High Street, Exeter EX4.
01392 431111

BOUTIQUES, DESIGNERS AND INDEPENDENT STORES

Duke's
Paul Street, Harlequin's Centre,
Exeter EX4. 01392 274840
Stylish store selling jeans, jewellery
and accessories, alongside
designer clothing by Armani and
Jean Muir.

Gardeners Clothing Company
32 Gandy Street, Exeter EX4.
01392 273155
Trendy little clothing store with an
emphasis on young casual fashion.

Garnish and Winkle
16 Gandy Street, Exeter EX4.
01392 428030
Designs from All Saints, Miss Sixty
and InWear.

Willy's
24 Gandy Street, Exeter EX4.
01392 490031
Lovely boutique selling Paul Smith,
Nolita, See by Chloé, Elisa Pensa,
Rutzou, Ghost, and Paige.

DEPARTMENT STORES

Dingles
35 High Street, Exeter EX4.
0870 1607241
Fashions by 7 For All Mankind,
Therapy, Coast, Oasis, Wallis,
Warehouse, Planet, and Olsen.
Also lingerie by Fantasie, Elle
Macpherson, Charnos and Calvin
Klein.

Debenhams
1–11 Sidwell Street, Exeter EX4.
0844 56 6161
Debenhams designs from Jasper
Conran, John Richmond and John
Rocha. Also concessions of Phase
Eight, Topshop, Wallis and
Principles.

VINTAGE

Enjoy Clothing
People's Palace, Pydar Street,
Truro TR1. 01872 262292
Women's clothing, shoes and
accessories from the 1940s
onwards. You can make some
excellent finds and stock changes
regularly. Open Thursday–Saturday,
10–5 pm.

Kitts Couture
51 Chapel Street, Penzance TR18.
01736 364507
www.kittscouture.co.uk
Wonderful vintage clothing from the
1920s–1970s. Have a look at the
fantastic website.

The Real McCoy
21 The Fore Street Centre, Fore
Street, Exeter EX4. 01392 410481
Vintage 20th-century clothing.

SALONS, SPAS AND BEAUTY STORES

Peppers
Musgrave House, Exeter EX4.
01392 274813
Guinot facials, glycolic peels and
anti-cellulite body peels, as well
as excellent hair care services.

Glasgow

HIGH STREET

All Saints
192 Ingram Street, Glasgow G1.
0141 248 6437

French Connection
Units 45–50, Princes Square, 48
Buchanan Street, Glasgow G1.
0141 248 7565

Jigsaw
177 Ingram Street, Glasgow G1.
0141 552 7639

Monsoon
17 Princes Square, Glasgow G1.
0141 221 8783

Oasis
The Glass House, Princes Square,
Buchanan Street, Glasgow G1
0141 248 8661

River Island
122–126 Sauchiehall Street,
Glasgow G2. 0141 332 2091

Topshop
Argyle Street, Glasgow G2.
0141 225 3467

Urban Outfitters
157 Buchanan Street, Glasgow G1.
0141 248 9203

Whistles
20–21 Princes Square, Buchanan
Street, Glasgow G1.
0141 226 5259

Zara
12 Buchanan Street, Glasgow G1.
0141 227 4770

BOUTIQUES, DESIGNERS AND INDEPENDENT STORES

Cruise
180 Ingram Street, Glasgow G1.
0141 572 3232
Seven floors of high fashion ranges,
including Alexander McQueen,
Fendi, Paul Smith, Armani, Prada,
Gucci, and Burberry.

Cruise Jeans
223 Ingram Street, Glasgow G1.
0141 229 0000
For more chilled-out fashion such
as Duffer, Fake London, Maharishi,
Prada Sport.

Moon
10 Ruthven Lane, Glasgow G12.
0141 339 2315
Fantastic boutique which sells the
excellent Megan Park collection.

Pringle
130 Buchanan Street, Glasgow G1.
0141 221 3434
Classic knits with a fashion edge.

DEPARTMENT STORES

House of Fraser
21–45 Buchanan Street, Glasgow
G1. 0870 1607243
Stocks Coast, DKNY, Fenn Wright
Manson, French Connection, Karen
Millen, and Linea.

John Lewis
220 Buchanan Street Glasgow G1.
0141 353 6677
Always excellent for hosiery, gloves
and trimmings. Stocks Hobbs, Paul
Costello, Kaliko, Phase Eight,
Warehouse, and Mexx.

VINTAGE

Flip
15 Bath Street, Glasgow G1.
0141 353 1634
Second-hand jeans and loads more
goodies to be found here.

Glorious
41 Ruthven Lane Byres Road,
Glasgow G12. 0141 357 5662
Second-hand designer fashions.

Mr Ben Vintage Clothing
Studio 6 Kings Court, 99 King
Street, Glasgow G1.
0141 553 1936
There's nothing like having a good
rummage and finding a true gem!

Retro Clothes
8 Otago Street, Kelvinbridge,
Glasgow G12. 0141 576 0165
Clothing from the 1950s and 60s.

SALONS, SPAS AND BEAUTY STORES

Jo Malone
25 Princes Square, 40 Buchanan
Street, Glasgow G1.
0141 847 0608
Fabulous scents, candles, bath
products and creams. Also facial
treatment rooms.

Space.NK
36–37 Princes Square, 48
Buchanan St, Glasgow G1.
0141 248 7931
Huge range of products and
treatments.

Revive Day Spa at Greens Health Club
141 Finnieston Street, Glasgow G3.
0844 414 2737
Dermalogica facials, Ionithermie
inch-loss treatments, massage and
luxurious treatment packages at
this modern spa set in smart health
club surroundings.

Leeds

HIGH STREET

Gap
135–137 Briggate, Leeds LS1.
0113 243 9414

Hobbs
6–8 Queen Victoria Street, Leeds
LS1. 0113 245 4014

Karen Millen
2 Queen Victoria Street, Leeds
LS1. 0113 244 6505

Kurt Geiger
9–11 Queen Victoria Street, Leeds
LS1. 0113 234 4953

Miss Selfridge
14–22 Lands Lane, Leeds LS1.
0113 246 7151

Oasis
115 Briggate, Leeds LS1.
0113 246 9019

Reiss
26-28 County Arcade, Leeds LS1.
0113 244 9040

Topshop
St Johns Centre, Leeds LS1.
0113 244 0475

Warehouse
Unit 4 Shopping Plaza, 22 Albion
Arcade, Leeds LS1. 0113 245
9431

Whistles
12–14 Queen Victoria Street, Leeds
LS1. 0113 243 9574

Zara
129–132 Briggate, Leeds LS1.
0113 380 4620

BOUTIQUES, DESIGNERS AND INDEPENDENT STORES

Accent
11–13 Queens Arcade, Leeds LS1.
0113 244 2414
Stocks Versace, Valentino, Replay
and the super-hip Nolita jeans.

Agent Provocateur
10 Queen Victoria Street, Leeds
LS1. 0113 243 3291
Sexy, sensuous, daring – and now
they have a maternity range.
Say it's not true!

Brora
10-12 Cross Arcade, Leeds LS1.
0113 244 6832
Beautiful cashmere clothing in wonderful colours and excellent quality.

Flannels
68–78 Vicar Lane, Leeds LS1.
0113 234 9977
Prada, Gucci, Chloé, etc. Lots of
smart labels and an excellent new
restaurant called Anthony's.

Formes
3-5 County Arcade, Leeds LS1.
0113 243 3456
Fashionable clothing to wear during
pregnancy.

Pollyanna Barnsley Ltd
14–16 Market Hill, Barnsley, South
Yorkshire S70. 01226 291665
www.pollyanna.com
This shop is not actually in Leeds,
but it's well worth the 15-mile
journey to visit one of the most
visionary fashions stores in Britain.
Here you will find Comme des
Garçons, Dries van Noten, Issey
Miyake, Junya Watanabe, YSL and
Yohji Yamamoto. Have a look at
their website too.

Room 7
64 Street Lane, Leeds LS13.
0113 236 9100
Stocks Dolce & Gabbana, Chloé,
Gucci, and Missoni, with accessories to match.

Sacred Hearts
8 County Arcade, Leeds LS1.
0113 247 0816
Beautiful lingerie, swimwear and
other goodies.

Size?
49-51 Vicar Lane, Leeds LS1.
0113 243 2221
The hippest trainers and casual
footwear. Stocks Converse, Adidas,
Nike and more.

Vivienne Westwood
15–17 County Arcade, Leeds LS1.
0113 245 6403
Small but perfectly formed branch
of this English designer's store.

DEPARTMENT STORES

Harvey Nichols
107–111 Briggate, Leeds LS1.
0113 204 8888
Fabulous miniature branch of HN,
which is overflowing with the best
of designer collections, including
Issa, Missoni, Temperley, Tory
Burch, Elie Tahari, Roberto Cavalli,
YSL, Pucci and Amanda Wakeley.
And there's a lovely café where you
can have delicious smoothies and
yummy lunches.

VINTAGE

Blue Rinse
9 & 11 Call Lane, Leeds LS1.
0113 245 1735
Second-hand Levi's, cords, jackets
and t-shirts.

Bubblegum Retro
9 Market Street, Hebden Bridge,
West Yorkshire HX7.
01422 847884
Vintage clothing and handbags
from the 1940s–1980s.

SALONS, SPAS AND BEAUTY STORES

Jo Malone
15-17 Queen Victoria Street, Leeds
LS1. 0113 245 5588
Wonderful facials and massages,
using the exquisite products.

Molton Brown
41 County Arcade, Leeds, LS1.
0113 242 6258
Bubble baths to travel essentials.

Rose & Co
22–24 County Arcade, Leeds LS1.
0113 245 4701
Old-fashioned apothecary with
beautifully packaged and scented
remedies. Wonderful skincare products from Burt's Bees and Dr.
Hauschka, and quirky homewares
reflecting the store's vintage style.

The Waterfall Spa
3 Brewery Wharf, Dock Street,
Leeds LS10. 0800 731 1995
Excellent day packages using in
house products. The most luxurious spa in the north of England.

Liverpool

HIGH STREET

French Connection
74 Lord Street, Liverpool L2.
0151 707 1115

Gap
99 Lord Street, Liverpool L2.
0151 236 7116

H&M
9–15 Church Street, Liverpool L1.
0151 703 2200

Kurt Geiger
Met Quarter, 35 Whitechapel,
Liverpool L1. 0151 255 0734

Monsoon
Unit 6–12, Clayton Square
Shopping Centre, Liverpool L1.
0151 707 8371

Oasis
10 Clayton Square, Liverpool L1.
0151 709 6862

Reiss
46 Stanley Street, Liverpool L1.
0151 227 9157

Topshop
22–36 Church Street, Liverpool L1.
0151 709 1160

Whistles
Met Quarter, Whitechapel, Liverpool
L1. 0151 227 9327

Zara
2–8 Church Street, Liverpool L1.
0151 702 6510

BOUTIQUES, DESIGNERS AND INDEPENDENT STORES

Cricket
Unit 9, Cavern Walks, Mathew
Street, Liverpool L2. 0151 227
4645
Stocks designers such as Missoni,
Pucci, Stella McCartney, Temperley,
Jenny Packham. Even a WAG can't
go wrong in this store.

Drome Couture
14 Cavern Walks, 8 Mathew Street,
Liverpool L2. 0151 255 0525
Dolce & Gabbana, Emanuel
Ungaro, Voyage Passion,
Blumarine, Roberto Cavalli, Gharani
Strok, 7 For All Mankind, Betsey
Johnson, Pringle Gold Label.

Drome Women
Cavern Walks, 8 Mathew Street,
Liverpool L2. 0151 258 1851
Evisu, Michiko Koshino, Custo,
Fornarina, Guess, Miss Sixty,
Diesel, Paul Frank, Nolita, Pringle,
Stussy, Baby Phat, Wale Adeyemi,
Dolce & Gabbana, Arrogant Cat.

Flannels
Met Quarter, Whitechapel, Liverpool
L1. 0151 236 0552
Large airy boutique stocking major
labels such as Prada, Gucci, Dolce
& Gabbana, Chloé and Cacharel.

DEPARTMENT STORES

John Lewis
20 Basnett Street, Liverpool L1.
0151 709 7070
Stockists of Coast, Fenn Wright
Manson, Jaeger, Liz Claiborne,
Mexx, Nougat, Paul Costelloe,
Warehouse, Kurt Geiger and Bertie.

VINTAGE

Bulletproof
41 Hardman Street, Liverpool L1.
0151 708 5808
Retro vintage clothing shop,
stocking original designs, mainly
jeans, coats and boots.

Pop Boutique
Quiggans Centre, School Lane,
Liverpool L1. 0151 707 0051
Vintage t-shirts, jeans and dresses

SALONS, SPAS AND BEAUTY STORES

MAC Cosmetics
Met Quarter, Whitechapel, Liverpool
L1. 0870 1925052
Fantastic make-up shop where all
the staff are make-up artists.
Experimenting with products and
colours is encouraged.

Molton Brown
Met Quarter, Whitechapel,
Liverpool L1.
0151 255 0497
Beautiful hair and bath products.
This branch also offers facial treat-
ments

Sassoon Studio
Met Quarter, 34 Whitechapel,
Liverpool L1.
0151 227 1450
Excellent hair care products
for sale.

London

HIGH STREET

All Saints
26 Kingly Street, London W1.
020 7494 3909

American Apparel
3–4 Carnaby Street, London W1.
020 7734 4477

Arrogant Cat
311 Kings Road, London SW3.
020 7349 9070

Coast
262–264 Regent Street, London
W1. 020 7287 9538

COS
222 Regent Street, London W1.
020 4780 401

Diesel
72 Kings Road, London SW3.
020 7225 3225

Evans
538 Oxford Street, London W1.
020 7499 0434

Faith
192–194 Oxford Street, London
W1. 020 7580 9561

French Connection
249–251 Regent Street, London
W1. 020 7493 3124

Gap
376–384 Oxford Street, London
W1. 020 7408 4500

H&M
481 Oxford Street, London W1.
020 7493 8557

Hobbs
124 Long Acre, London WC2.
020 7836 0625

Jigsaw
192 Westbourne Grove, London
W11. 020 7229 8654

Karen Millen
22-23 James Street, London WC2.
020 7836 5355

Kurt Geiger
65 South Molton Street, London
W1. 020 7758 8020

Lee
14 Carnaby Street, London W1.
020 7434 0732

Levi's
174–176 Regent Street, London
W1. 020 7292 2500

Marks & Spencer
458 Oxford Street, London W1.
020 7935 7954

Miss Selfridge
Ground Floor, 36–38 Great Castle
Street, London W1 020 7927 0214

Miss Sixty
39 Neal Street, London WC2.
020 7836 3789

Monsoon
5-6 James Street, London WC2.
020 7379 3623

Nine West
90 Kings Road, London SW3.
020 7581 7044

Oasis
12–14 Argyll Street, London W1.
020 7434 1799

Office
16 Carnaby Street, London W1.
020 7434 2530

Primark
499-517 Oxford Street, London
W1. 020 7495 0420

Principles
260 Regent Street, London W1.
020 7287 3365

River Island
301 Oxford Street, London W1.
020 7493 1431

Russell & Bromley
24–25 New Bond Street, London
W1. 020 7629 6903

Ted Baker
19 Duke Of York Square, London
SW3. 020 7881 0850

Topshop
216 Oxford Street, London W1.
020 7636 7700

Urban Outfitters
7 Dials Warehouse, London WC2.
020 7759 6390

Whistles
12–14 Christopher's Place, London
W1. 020 7487 4484

Zara
118 Regent Street, London W1.
020 7534 9500

BOUTIQUES, DESIGNERS AND INDEPENDENT STORES

Agnes b
35–36 Floral Street, London WC2.
020 7379 1992
Chic French separates, dresses
and shoes. Classic white shirts.

Aimé
32 Ledbury Road, London W11.
020 7221 7070
A French lifestyle boutique stocking
Isabel Marant, Les Prairies de
Paris, APC, and fabulous new label
Madame à Paris. Shoes, boots and
bags by Isabel Marant and APC.
Ballet pumps by Repetto. Designer
Jewellery by Serge Thoraval and
Aurélie Bidermann. Great range of
candles too.

Betsey Johnson
29 Floral Street, London WC2.
020 7240 6164
Another hidden gem, fabulous
party dresses and very cool
accessories.

Brora
344 Kings Road, London SW3.
020 7736 9944
Delicious cashmere in every colour.

Browns
South Molton Street, London W1
020 7514 0016
Ever-expanding designer store
stocking Marni, Missoni, Vanessa
Bruno, Jil Sander, Dosa,
Balenciaga. There is also an excel-
lent shoe department in the back.

London

Browns Focus
38–39 South Molton Street,
London W1. 020 7514 0064
Downstairs is a fashionable jeans
shop with denim from Chloé,
Superfine, Acne Jeans, and Sass
& Bide. Upstairs is high-fashion
clothing from Marc by Marc
Jacobs, See by Chloé, Lutz,
and Vanessa Bruno.

Coco Ribbon
21 Kensington Park Road, London
W11. 020 7229 4904
Sweet romantic boutique. Feminine
and frilly – great for presents.

Diane von Furstenberg
83 Ledbury Road, London W11.
020 7221 1120
Stylish designer dress shop that's
well worth a visit. Beautiful fabrics,
flattering styles, including the
signature wrap dress and maternity
range.

Dover Street Market
17–18 Dover Street, London W1.
020 7518 0680
This extraordinary store spread
over five floors in Mayfair gives us
a chance to look closely at cutting-
edge fashions, normally seen only
on high fashion catwalks, close up
and under one roof. Lanvin, Nina
Ricci, Alaia, Junya Watanabe and
Comme Des Garçons all show here
and there is a very chic café on the
top floor where you can sit and
read obscure fashion magazines.
While pretty much everything in this
shop is expensive, the atmosphere
is all about inspiration and aesthetic
– and the staff are very extremely
friendly and welcoming.

Egg
36 & 37 Kinnerton Street, London
SW1. 020 72359315
Italian Daniela Gregis took over the
main clothing line. Think floaty but
crisp, comfortable, sharp pieces in
the best linens, cottons, and silks.
The second line, made by Tibetans,
transcends time and fashion.

Iris
73 Salisbury Road, Queens Park,
London NW6. 020 7372 1777
Gorgeous feminine boutique stock-
ing Vanessa Bruno, Tania, Malene
Birger, Antik Batik and Cacharel.
Also lingerie by Elle Macpherson,
Hush, Cosebella, and Spank.
A true hidden gem.

Jaeger
200–206 Regent Street, London
W1. 020 7200 4015
Recently revamped, Jaeger has a
few fantastic pieces each season.

Hoxton Boutique
2 Hoxton Street, London N1.
020 7684 2083
Stocks their own divine +HOBO+
range of clothing and many other
cutting-edge styles in fashion and
accessories, including Isabel
Marant, Antoni & Alison,
Minimarket, and Repetto.

Koh Samui
65–67 Monmouth Street, London
WC2. 020 7240 4280
This store gets the best of the best
every season – Chloé, Vanessa
Bruno, Marc Jacobs, Balenciaga,
Paul & Joe, Ann Louise Roswald,
and much, much more. The shop
sells shoes, bags and accessories
as well as selected perfumes, jewellery and hand-picked vintage
clothing. They often have key
pieces from design collections long
before the department stores and
their prices are the best in London
for the products they carry. If you
can't quite afford the full cost, then
visit during the sale times when the
very generous discounts make a
huge difference.

Laundry Industry
186 Westbourne Grove, London
W11. 020 7792 7967
The shop's layout is like going in to
a time machine. Fab dresses.

Matches
60–64 Ledbury Road, London
W11. 020 7221 0255
If you would like to walk up Sloane
Street visiting all the shops, but you
just don't have the time, Matches
select fine pieces from all the major
designers – Chloé, Stella
McCartney, Prada, Martin Margiela,
Marc Jacobs, Balenciaga and
Lanvin – and put them under one
roof. They have shoes, bags, lovely
staff and free champagne to help
you feel the fear and buy it anyway.

Matches Spy
85 Ledbury Road, London W11.
020 7221 2334
Matches' little sister boutique. Miu
Miu, 3.1 Phillip Lim, Martin Margiela
Line 6, and Marc by Marc Jacobs
are all stocked here, along with a
range of really desirable shoes. The
average spend here would be
around £250, which will feel like a
bargain if you have just looked in
grown up Matches across the road.

Marc Jacobs
24–25 Mount Street, London W1.
020 7399 1690
London's brand new flagship store
for this maverick designer focuses
on the more expensive Marc
Jacobs line and the ever popular
handbag range. The Marc Jacobs
scents are divine and there is also a
selection of cool t-shirts.

MiMi
309 Kings Road, London SW3.
020 7349 9699
Colourful boutique with an emphasis on evening styles: ranges
include Marc Jacobs, Gharani
Strok and Collette Dinnigan. Shoes
from Jimmy Choo and Christian
Louboutin.

Miu Miu
123 New Bond Street, London W1.
020 7409 0900
This designer shop consistently
produces the best shoes of each
season every season. Witty wearable fashions from Miuccia Prada.

Orla Kiely
31 Monmouth Street, London
WC2. 020 7240 4022
Brightly coloured coats and
patterned shift dresses hanging
next to fabulous luggage, handbags, wellies, and accessories.
She even does chocolates in boxes
with her signature print – delicious!

Paul & Joe
39-41 Ledbury Road, London
W11. 020 7243 5510
This designer really came into her
own this season and key pieces
sold out in days. Very chic and not
too expensive in comparison to
some top designers. They have
a Paul & Joe Sister label, which is
really affordable.

Start
42–44 Rivington Street, London
EC2. 020 7729 3334
Miu Miu, Issa and lots of super-
trendy jeans. Very, very hip urban
feel to most of the clothes and
shoes stocked here. Perfume,
make-up and skincare also available. The lovely pug dogs are
unfortunately not for sale.

Shop at Maison Bertaux
27 Greek Street, London W1.
05601 151584
The only boutique in London that's
in a cake shop. This fantastic store
stocks APC, Eley Kishimoto and
Sonia Rykiel, along with beautiful
shoes, jewellery, sunglasses and
scented candles.

Souvenir
53 Brewer Street, London W1.
020 7287 8708
Fabulous little store crammed with
Vivienne Westwood, Victor & Rolf,
Hussein Chalayan, and Prairie
New York.

The Cross
141 Portland Road, London W11.
020 7727 6760
Dosa, Pearl Lowe, Sara Berman,
and Velvet. Lovely cashmere cardi-
gans, shoes, jewellery and bags –
you never will be able to leave
empty handed. Simply divine
clothing.

The West Village
44 Monmouth Street, London
WC2. 020 7240 7835
This company seems to make
the same dress over and over in
various different jersey prints, but
there are many other pretty dresses
and coats, and lots of crochet
styles in this boho boutique .

DESIGNER SHOES

Christian Louboutin
23 Motcomb Street, London SW1.
020 7245 6510
Extraordinary French shoes with
signature red soles.

Iris
61 Ledbury Road, London W11.
020 7229 1870
Lovely shoe boutique, stocking
shoes from Chloé, Marc Jacobs
and other high-end designers.
What is brilliant is that they carry
pretty much the whole range of
shoes and no other store does
that.

Jimmy Choo
27 New Bond Street, London W1.
020 7823 1051
Glamorous red carpet styles and
super-tight sexy boots.

Patrick Cox
129 Sloane Street, London SW1.
020 7730 8886
Great styles abound in this
exclusive Chelsea shoe shop.

Post Mistress
61–63 Monmouth Street, London,
WC2. 020 7379 4040
Fantastic shoe store in Covent
Garden sells Ugg boots, L'Autre
Chose, Birkenstocks, Dries van
Noten, Miu Miu, Vivienne
Westwood, Belstaff and many
more.

Manolo Blahnik
49-51 Old Church Street, London
SW3. 020 7352 8622
Some of the most elegant shoes in
the world have been crafted by
Manolo. Truly desirable footwear.

Mootich
34 Elizabeth Street, London SW1.
020 7824 8113
This great shop sells unusual but
very wearable boots and shoes.

Tods
35–36 Sloane Street, London SW1.
020 7235 1320
Popular, comfortable, long-lasting
styles in shoes and bags.

HOSIERY

Fogal
3a Sloane Street, London SW1.
020 7235 3115
Every possible colour of tights
and stockings.

Tabio
94 Kings Road, London SW3.
020 7591 1960
The most fabulous sock and tight
shop ever. Looking for unusual
colours? This is the shop for you.

Wolford
3 South Molton Street, London W1.
020 7499 2549
The best opaque tights in the
universe.

LINGERIE

Rigby & Peller
2 Hans Road, London SW3.
020 7235 0229
Bras that fit perfectly. Seriously
good underwear.

Agent Provocateur
6 Broadwick Street, London W1.
020 7439 0229
Sometimes bordering on camp but
amazing anyway. This is the original
sexy lingerie store.

Bravissimo
20 Tavistock Street, London WC2.
0845 4081907
Fantastic selection of glamorous
lingerie and swimwear for large-
breasted women. Call ahead to
pre-book fitting appointments if
you're planning to visit the shop
at busy times.

London

Myla
74 Duke of York Square, London
SW3. 020 7730 0700
Pretty lingerie.

Coco De Mer
23 Monmouth Street, London
WC2. 020 7836 8882
Saucy lingerie.

DEPARTMENT STORES

Harrods
Knightsbridge, London SW1.
020 7730 1234
The most famous department store
of all. Harrods is a day out – if you
forget what you came for you could
disappear in here until closing time.
They have an excellent shoe
department carrying a huge selection of designer brands, including
Prada, Dior, Chanel, Louis Vuitton,
Chloé and Lanvin. There is a
slightly conservative air among the
collections, though they sell Marni,
Dolce & Gabbana, Prada, Chloé,
Givenchy and of course many less
expensive designers as well.

Harvey Nichols
109–125 Knightsbridge, London
SW1 020 7235 5000
Wonderfully compact fashion
emporium on the corner of
Knightsbridge. Stockists of Miu
Miu, Balenciaga, Chloé, Stella
McCartney, Burberry Prosum,
Givenchy, Lanvin and Jimmy Choo,
as well as a less expensive range of
designers on the 3rd floor, including
3.1 Phillip Lim, Paul & Joe, Marc by
Marc Jacobs, Vanessa Bruno, See
by Chloé, and Cacharel. Fantastic
beauty and perfume hall.
Restaurants and coffee bars
upstairs.

Liberty
Great Marlborough Street, London
W1 020 75739484
Probably London's most beautiful
store. There is an amazing perfume
department on the ground floor.
Women's fashions on the 1st floor
carry the best selection of Vivienne
Westwood clothing in town as well
as Gharani Strok, APC, Issa, Marc
by Marc Jacobs, and See by
Chloé. The designer room sells
Westwood Gold Label, Martin
Margiella, Alexander McQueen,
Missoni, Anne Valerie Hash, Ann
Demeulemeester and Rick Owens,
and there is a good vintage
boutique. Lovely bath and bedtime
section upstairs. Cream teas with
rose jam available on the ground
and third floor. Not much in the way
of knickers but lovely all the same.

Selfridges
400 Oxford Street, W1. 0870
8377377
The behemoth of style, Selfridges
fashion halls are large and overwhelming at times. It's easy to get
lost but worth persevering as they
stock an enormous range of clothing from the high-street section on
the ground floor with Topshop,
Warehouse, Oasis and French
Connection, to super-hip Miu Miu,
Theory, Alexander McQueen,
Burberry, Fendi, Dries van Noten,
Joseph, Armani, Paul Smith, DKNY,
Diane von Furstenberg and the
largest selection of Marc by Marc
Jacobs in London. Gucci, Chloé,
Marni and Balenciaga all have
concessions here. The lingerie
selection is the biggest and best in
town and the shoe department is
excellent as well. If you love your
labels you'll want to pay a visit.

VINTAGE/MARKETS

Annie's Vintage Costume
12 Camden Passage, London N1.
020 7359 0796
Lots of white lace and vintage silk
slips and French cotton. Wonderful
antique market opens every weekend, though there is plenty to see
in Camden Passage on any day
of the week.

Blackout II
51 Endell Street, London WC2.
020 7240 5006
From the 20s through to the 80s.

Camden Market
Between Camden Underground
and Chalk Farm Underground
stations. Sundays
Enormous weekend market. Almost
everything is available here, includ-
ing a few things that shouldn't be!
Check out the newly developed
Camden Lock and The Stables
Market.

Camden Passage Antiques
Market
Camden Passage, London N1.
Weekend antiques market. Lots of
stalls selling vintage clothing and
bric-a-brac.

Grays Antique Markets
1–7 Davies Street, London W1.
020 7235 5000
All sorts of collectables – antique
lace, extra-special high-end
vintage, shoes, and so much more.
You need a day to get round this
place!

One of a Kind
253 Portobello Road, London W11.
020 7792 5284
A real treasure trove of vintage
goodies, but the prices could make
you faint…

Orsini
76 Earls Court Road, London W8.
020 7937 0203
Beautiful but expensive vintage
clothing. Some real collectors'
items to be found here.

Pop Boutique
6 Monmouth Street London WC2.
020 7497 5262
Specialist in 70s and 80s retro chic.

Portobello Market
Portobello Road, London W11.
World famous and rightly so. Runs
from dawn till dusk on Friday and
Saturday, with a smaller selection
of stalls under the Westway on
Sunday. Antiques, vintage, new
clothes, bags, jewellery, everything
anyone could ever need – fantastic
atmosphere.

Relik
8 Golborne Road, London W10.
020 8962 0089
The best ever vintage shop. If you are stuck for something to wear it's guaranteed you'll find something here.

Rokit
101 Brick Lane, London E1.
020 7375 3864
Very chic, urban cool clothing with a touch of grunge. Specialises in clothing from the 70s – cowboy boots and other fabulous things.

Spitalfields Market
Between Liverpool Street Station and Brick Lane. Sundays 11–6pm. Young designers, independent artisans, modern and vintage clothing.

Steinberg & Tolkien
193 Kings Road, London SW3.
020 7376 3660
Best for beautiful, rare and expensive collectables.

Virginia
98 Portland Road, London W11.
020 7727 9908
This wonderful shop looks like the boudoir of the bride of Dracula – lovely silk slips, lots of lace. Call ahead as the shop is often closed for photo shoots!

SALONS, SPAS AND BEAUTY STORES

Angela Flanders Perfumer
96 Columbia Road, London E2.
020 7739 7555
Open Sunday, 9.30–2.30, and Monday–Thursday by appointment. Extraordinary perfumes, lotions and candles, also available at Precious 16 Artillery Passage, London E1.

Bliss
60 Sloane Avenue, London SW7.
020 7584 3888
Condé Nast Traveler's Spa of the Year 2007. Gorgeous treatments, including the Triple Oxygen Facial, Shrink Wrap and Deep Sea Detox for the body. Fantastic range of products to take away.

Elemis Day Spa
2–3 Lancashire Court, London W1.
0870 4104210
Exotic and luxurious treatments in central London.

Eve Lom
2 Spanish Place, London W1.
020 7935 9988
The original fabulous facial.

Nadia Nicholas
325 Fulham Road, London SW10.
020 7352 6285
Extraordinary lymphatic facials and body treatments using natural products, many made by Nadia herself. Try the Intwine therapy, a personalised face and body treatment designed to meet the needs of each individual client.

Origins
42 Neal St, London WC2.
020 7836 9603
Excellent face and body care products.

Relax
65–67 Brewer Street, London W1.
020 7494 3333
All kinds of massage in bright, airy, modern surroundings – walk-in chair massages, full body aromatherapy massages, shiatsu, deep tissue etc.

Richard Ward Hair & Metrospa
82 Duke Of York Square, London SW3 020 7730 1222
Our absolute favourite hairdresser!

Space.NK
131 Westbourne Grove, London W2. 020 7727 8002
Fabulous beauty store selling Nars, Laura Mercier, Diptyque, and a multitude of other lotions and potions. This large branch has treatment rooms attached so you can indulge in a massage or facial.

The Cowshed
119 Portland Road, London W11.
020 7078 1944
Huge selection of tempting treatments, vitamin-C facials and fruit acid pedicures. The food menu is a lure in itself.

The Organic Pharmacy
169 Kensington High Street, London W8. 020 7376 9200
Delicious but pricey products with no harmful additives.

Manchester

HIGH STREET

All Saints
52 King Street, Manchester M2.
0161 832 2444

French Connection
Kings Court, 2–4 Exchange Street,
Manchester M2. 0161 835 1727

Jigsaw
Triangle Site, Exchange Square,
Manchester M4. 0161 833 3304
With its own restaurant, 'Jigsaw
Kitchen'

Kurt Geiger
7 Exchange Street, Manchester
M2. 0161 832 9270

Mango
48–50 Market Street, Manchester
M1 0161 835 9097

Oasis
50 King St, Manchester, M2.
0161 839 4735

Office
16 St Ann's Square, Manchester
M2. 0161 832 7337

Shoes by Topshop
20–22 King Street, Manchester M2.
0161 832 5404
The only Topshop store in the UK
dedicated to shoes.

Urban Outfitters
42–43 Market Street, Manchester
M1. 0161 8176640

Whistles
55 King Street, Manchester M2.
0161 8395399

Zara
Unit 2, The Shambles, New
Cathedral Street, Manchester M1.
0161 831 0940

BOUTIQUES, DESIGNERS AND INDEPENDENT STORES

Agent Provocateur
81 King Street, Manchester M2.
0161 833 3735
Lingerie heaven…

Arc
15a Corporation Street,
Manchester M4. 0161 839 6391
Young boutique selling jeans,
t-shirts and ranges such as Bench
and Carhart

Flannels
4 St Ann's Place, St Ann's Square,
Manchester M2.
0161 832 5536
Very smart women's wear: Gucci,
Prada, Dolce & Gabbana, Versace
and Matthew Williamson.

Flannels
55 King Street, Manchester M2.
0161 839 7824
Less expensive sister store, stocking Miu Miu, Malene Birger, Paul
Smith, and Flannels' own range.

Mulberry
62 King Street, Manchester M2.
0161 839 3333
Delicious handbags at eye-watering
prices. but oh so worth it!

Vivienne Westwood
47 Spring Gardens, Manchester
M2. 0161 835 2121
The ultimate in sexy tailoring.

DEPARTMENT STORES

Harvey Nichols
21 New Cathedral Street,
Manchester M1. 0161 828 8888
Fantastic branch of this smart
department store, carrying collec-
tions from many of the top names
in fashion, including Vera Wang
Lavender, Lanvin, Dries van Noten,
Diane von Furstenberg, Balenciaga,
3.1 by Phillip Lim, Marc by Marc
Jacobs, Paul Smith and Matthew
Williamson.

Selfridges
1 Exchange Square, Manchester
M3. 0870 837 7377
Stockists of nearly everything,
including Versace, Paul Smith,
Dolce & Gabbana, Alexander
McQueen, Maharishi, Stella
McCartney, Moschino, See by
Chloé, DKNY, Miu Miu, plus a
range of exciting designer footwear,
accessories, and excellent make-
up and perfume hall.

VINTAGE/MARKETS

Aflex Palace
52 Church Street, Manchester M4.
0161 832 3839
Large eclectic clothing market.
Vintage, one-off pieces, young
designers, accessories and tons
more.

Origins at Oxfam
Oldham Street, Manchester M1.
0161 839 3160
Recycle, get great clothes and be
ethical all at the same time – how
fab is that?

Pop Boutique
36 Oldham Street, Manchester M1.
0161 236 5797
Excellent boutique selling their own
range of clothing alongside vintage
pieces from the 1960s, 70s and
80s.

Rags to Bitches
60 Tib Street, Manchester M4.
0161 835 9265
A wide range of vintage items,
some from as far back as the
1920s through to 1980s.

SALONS, SPAS AND BEAUTY STORES

Nicky Clarke
The Triangle, Manchester M4.
0161 833 3555
One of Britain's most famous hair-
dressers has opened a salon in
Manchester. Excellent colour and
cuts, using his own signature styling
products.

Space.NK
The Corn Exchange, Manchester
Triangle, Manchester M4.
0161 832 6220
Yummy products and fabulous
make-up.

The Lowry Spa
The Lowry Hotel, 50 Dearman's
Place, Manchester M6.
0161 827 4034
Offering luxurious and unique
treatments and therapies, including
Carita, Espa and Ishi.

Newcastle

HIGH STREET

All Saints
33 Market Street, Newcastle NE1.
0191 221 1320

French Connection
155 Grainger Street, Newcastle
NE1. 0191 221 2193

Jigsaw
151 Grainger Street, Newcastle
NE1. 0191 261 4715

Karen Millen
29–39 Market Street, Newcastle
NE1. 0191 261 6185

Monsoon
Eldon Square Shopping Centre,
Newcastle NE1. 0191 260 2693

Oasis
35 Market Street, Newcastle NE1.
0191 261 6812

Primark
78 Northumberland Street,
Newcastle NE1. 0191 261 5093

Ravel
7 Eldon Way, Eldon Square,
Newcastle NE1. 0191 232 5048

Reiss
133 Grainger Street, Newcastle
NE1. 0191 230 4999

Zara
Units 9 & 10 Metrocentre,
Gateshead, Newcastle.
0191 493 3580

BOUTIQUES, DESIGNERS AND INDEPENDENT STORES

Ophelia Boutique
11 & 12 Clayton Road, Newcastle
NE2. 0191 281 0609
Lingerie, swimwear, lounge wear
and lots of other gorgeous things.
Stocks CashCa, extraordinary
cashmere garments, La Perla, Fleur
T and Agent Provocateur perfumes.

Wolford
Eldon Gardens, Newcastle NE1.
0191 232 2288
Probably the best opaque tights on
the planet, plus lingerie, body wear
and swimwear.

DEPARTMENT STORES

Fenwick
41 Windsor Terrace, Newcastle
NE3. 0191 2851202
DKNY, Nicole Farhi, Ralph Lauren,
Joseph, Maxmara, Max & Co, 7
For All Mankind, Sticky Fingers,
Coast, Whistles, Karen Millen.

VINTAGE

Attica
2 George Yard, Newcastle NE1.
0191 261 4062
Turn-of-the-century period clothing
through to 1970s.

Retro Modern
29 Highbridge, Newcastle NE1.
0191 232 5514
Clothing and accessories from the
1960s onwards.

Royal Vintage
4a Worswick Street, Newcastle
NE1. 0191 230 3040
Collection of clothing from
1970s–1990s.

SALONS, SPAS AND BEAUTY STORES

The Serenity Spa
Seaham Hall Hotel, Lord Byron's
Walk, Seaham, County Durham.
0191 516 1550
Exotic spa just 20 minutes from
Newcastle, this has thermal baths,
steam rooms and offers a range of
treatments, including Elemis Aroma
Stone Therapy.

Space.NK
132 Grainger Street, Newcastle
NE1. 0191 260 3251
The most fabulous products, the
perfect place to pamper yourself.

Norwich

HIGH STREET

Gap
30 London Street, Norwich NR2.
01603 624895

H&M
The Mall, Norwich NR2.
01603 621551

Jaeger
31 London Street, Norwich NR2.
01603 622821

Karen Millen
10 London Street, Norwich NR2.
01603 762282

Miss Selfridge
22 St Stephen's Street, Norwich
NR1. 01603 626803

Oasis
36 Castle Mall, Norwich NR1.
01603 612656

Russell & Bromley
21 London Street, Norwich NR2.
01603 619818

TK Maxx
Castle Mall Shopping Centre,
Norwich NR1. 01603 762115

Topshop
15–17 Haymarket, Norwich NR2.
01603 626154

Zara
Unit 3, Merchant Hall, Chapel Field,
Norwich NR1. 01603 671750

BOUTIQUES, DESIGNERS AND INDEPENDENT STORES

Ginger Ladies Wear
35 Timber Hill, Norwich NR1.
01603 763158
Fashionable boutique stocking
Armani Jeans, Paul Smith, Ted
Baker, Juicy Couture, Ralph
Lauren, D&G.

Le Creme
39 Exchange Street, Norwich NR2.
01603 628881
Smart designer shop. Includes
good formal wear from Ian Stewart,
Jenny Packham.

Raffles
16 Timber Hill, Norwich NR1.
01603 766100
Lovely shoe shop selling styles
from Moda in Pelle, Capollini and
many more.

Two Stars
10 Royal Arcade, Norwich NR2.
01603 764671
Megan Park, Marilyn Moore, 120%
Linen, Orla Kiely, and Velvet.

Ursula's Lingerie
25 Timberhill, Norwich, NR1.
01603 664255
Indulge yourself with some
gorgeous lingerie.

DEPARTMENT STORES
Jarrold
5 London Street, Norwich NR2.
01603 660661
Independent department store with
an excellent selection of women's
clothing. Collections from Coast,
Episode, Phase Eight, French
Connection, Nicole Farhi, Nougat,
Max Mara Weekend, Fenn Wright
Manson, Jaeger and Betty Barclay.
The lingerie department also has
many popular brands including
DKNY, Aubade, Beau Bra, Triumph
and Fantasie.

House of Fraser
130 Merchants Hall, Chapelfield
Shopping Centre, Norwich NR2.
0870 160 7259
Dune, Office, French Connection,
Zara, Mango and Monsoon.

VINTAGE

Past Caring
6 Chapel Yard Holt, Norfolk NR25.
01263 713771
Clothes from the Victorian era to
1960s.

SALONS, SPAS AND BEAUTY STORES

Sprowston Manor Hotel Spa
Sprowston Park, Wroxham Road,
Norwich NR7. 01603 410871
Luxury spa in an imposing country
hotel set in acres of grounds.
The spa offers various treatments
using Espa products.

Nottingham

HIGH STREET

All Saints
3 Thurland Street, Nottingham
NG1. 0115 941 7150

Faith
Unit 48, The Victoria Centre,
Nottingham NG1. 0115 950 9833

H&M
11 Lister Gate, Nottingham NG1.
0115 852 3760

Jigsaw
21-23 Bridlesmith Gate,
Nottingham NG1. 0115 941 4437

Karen Millen
15 Exchange Arcade, Nottingham
NG1. 0115 947 2898

Kurt Geiger
29 Bridlesmith Gate, Nottingham
NG1. 0115 950 4518

Reiss
5 Byard Lane, Nottingham NG1.
0115 950 1025

River Island
11-17 Lister Gate, Nottingham
NG1. 0115 958 1191

Topshop
122-123 Victoria Centre
Nottingham NG1. 0115 948 3026

Whistles
3-7 Middle Pavement, Nottingham
NG1. 0115 9475551

BOUTIQUES, DESIGNERS AND INDEPENDENT STORES

Bravissimo
11 Pelham Street, Nottingham
NG1. 0845 4081910
Great lingerie and swimwear for
big-boobed women. 20-minute
fitting appointments available.

Cruise Flannels
36 Bridlesmith Gate, Nottingham
NG1. 0115 947 6466
Stocks Prada, Gucci, Jil Sander,
Ghost and Comme des Garçons.

Limeys
58 Bridlesmith Gate, Nottingham
NG1. 0115 958 4097
Collections from Juicy Couture,
Superfine, Velvet, Nanette Lepore,
Hugo Boss and L'Autre Chose.

Paul Smith
Willoughby House, 20 Low
Pavement, Nottingham NG1.
0115 968 5990
The designer's store in his home
town has English women's wear
in his signature style.

Siren Lingerie
10 Flying Horse Walk, Nottingham
NG1. 0115 985 9991
From La Perla to Rigby & Peller and
many more.

DEPARTMENT STORES

House of Fraser
2 Union Road, Nottingham NG1.
0870 160 7273
Ghost, Laundry, Nicole Farhi,
Untold, Whistles, Oska, Joseph,
Hobbs and contemporary
collections from Firetrap, Hooch,
Therapy, French Connection, Ted
Baker and Kookai, with shoes by
Roland Cartier, Marc Jacobs, Pied
à Terre and Bertie.

John Lewis
Victoria Centre, Nottingham NG1.
0115 941 8282
Stocks Coast, Hobbs, Kaliko,
Phase Eight. Also has excellent
ranges of lingerie and hosiery.

VINTAGE

Celia's Vintage Clothing
66-68 Derby Road, Nottingham
NG1. 0115 947 3036
Period Victorian pieces through
to 1980s.

Kathleen & Lily's
205 Mansfield Road, Nottingham
NG1. 0115 941 2327
Clothes from the 1940s–1980s.

SALONS, SPAS AND BEAUTY STORES

Joshua Tree Aveda Concept Hair Salon & Spa Roko Health Club
Wilford Lane, West Bridgeford,
Nottingham NG2. 0115 981 3111
Unblock your chakras with an
Ayurvedic massage or indulge in
excellent hair and beauty treat-
ments using Aveda products.
Luxurious surroundings. Reiki and
reflexology also available.

MAC Cosmetics
14 Cheapside, Nottingham NG1.
0115 985 9413
The mecca for make-up.

Saks Hair & Beauty
215 Drury Walk, Broadmarsh
Centre, Nottingham NG8.
0115 947 2467
Try Saks Sensory Heaven for the
complete pampering experience.
Includes a head and body massage
with skin specific facial.

Toni & Guy
4 Cheapside, Nottingham NG1.
0115 9415756
Up-to-the-minute cuts and colour.

Oxford

HIGH STREET

Dolcis
14 The Clarendon Centre,
Cornmarket Street, Oxford OX1.
01865 240532

Dorothy Perkins
9-10 Queen Street, Oxford OX1.
01865 246685

Jigsaw
133 High Street, Oxford OX1.
01865 240820

Hobbs
115 High Street, Oxford OX1.
01865 249437

Karen Millen
136 High Street, Oxford OX1.
01865 246386

Monsoon
35 Queen Court, Oxford OX1.
01865 240685

Oasis
37 St Ebbes Street, Oxford OX1.
01865 200722

Primark
27 Westgate, Oxford OX1.
01865 248072

River Island
The Clarendon Centre, Cornmarket
Street Oxford OX1. 01865 242662

Russell & Bromley
St Michael's Mansions, 3 Ship
Street, Oxford OX1. 01865 240200

Topshop
1 Magdalen Street, Oxford OX1.
01865 723709

Whistles
9 High Street, Oxford OX1.
01865 728446

Zara
The Clarendon Centre, Cornmarket
Street, Oxford OX1. 01865 208700

BOUTIQUES, DESIGNERS AND INDEPENDENT STORES

Agnes b
90 High Street, Oxford OX1.
01865 245444
Chic French designer clothing.

Bajan Blue
50 High Street, Oxford OX1.
01865 248024
Designer swimwear from Melissa
Odabash, Miraclesuit@figleaves
and DKNY in sizes up to a G-cup.

Brora
131 High Street, Oxford OX1.
01865 243787
Soft, colourful cashmere clothing
and accessories.

Plum
34 Walton Street, Oxford OX2.
01865 511345
Stockists of Joseph, Miss Sixty,
Nicole Farhi and Nougat.

Lizzy James
Little Clarendon Street, Oxford
OX1. 01865 512936
Armani, DKNY and many more.

Lolapoloza Blue
Boar Street, Oxford OX1.
01865 205073
Exclusive handbags and jewellery
alongside art in this attractive
gallery.

Sassi
55 The High Street, Oxford OX1.
01865 205151
Fashionable styles from designer
ranges such as L'Autre Chose and
Barbara Bui.

DEPARTMENT STORES

Debenhams
1 Magdalen Street, Oxford OX1.
0870 6003333

VINTAGE

Bead Games
40 Crowley Road, Littlemore,
Oxford OX4.
01865 251620
1950s–1980s vintage clothing

Uncle Sam's
25 Little Clarendon Street,
Oxford OX1.
01865 510759
American vintage clothing.

Unicorn
Ship Street, Oxford OX1.
Full of dresses, shoes and
dressing-up outfits from
1940s-1970s.

SALONS, SPAS AND BEAUTY STORES

The Tao Beauty Salon
99 St Aldates, Oxford OX1.
01865 249347
Established salon offering a variety
of beauty treatments, massage
and therapies, including reiki,
Indian head massage and Hopi
ear candles.

Toni & Guy
21 George Street, Oxford OX1.
01865 241000
Contemporary cuts and excellent
haircare products.

Shopping Malls

The huge growth in purpose-built shopping cities has contributed to the death of the high street. Many chain stores close down smaller regional branches and concentrate resources on larger, out of town shopping centres. Independent stores feel the pinch as shoppers head out of town to spend money at these one-stop destinations. While it is undoubtedly sad to see once bustling high streets reduced to lacklustre, half-empty discount alleys, the fact is that these giant retail centres would not be thriving if they were not extremely popular with the shopping public. Most centres have larger branches of high street favourites, offering more stock in more sizes – so less chance of disappointment. There are bathrooms – difficult to find on the average UK high street and essential, particularly when shopping with children. Nearly all centres have free and abundant parking, also increasingly rare in Britain. There are plenty of restaurants and cafés and, even if they're rather bland, it's somewhere to leave the husband and kids while you shop.

Bicester Village
50 Pingle Drive, Oxfordshire OX26. 01869 323200
www.bicestervillage.com
Fantastic designer outlet village with discount ranges from designers and the best of the high street. Stores include Burberry, Jigsaw, Calvin Klein, Max Mara, Hugo Boss, Dior, Cath Kidston, Diesel, Jaeger, Furla, Versace, Tods, Celine, Mulberry, Myla, Ted Baker, Polo Ralph Lauren, French Connection, Nicole Farhi, Whistles and lots more.

Bluewater
Greenhithe, Kent DA9. 0870 7770252. www.bluewater.co.uk
Stores include Armani Exchange, Accessorize, Aldo, All Saints, Bay Trading Company, The Body Shop, Crabtree & Evelyn, Calvin Klein Jeans, Clarks, Coast, Diesel, Dune, Dolcis, East, Evans, Joseph, John Lewis, Jigsaw, Jaeger, Kew, Karen Millen, La Senza, L'Occitane, LK Bennett, Levi's, Miss Selfridge, Molton Brown (with day spa) Mikey, Mango, Marks & Spencer, Monsoon, New Look, Oasis, Nine West, Reiss, Russell & Bromley, Republic, Wallis, Wolford and Zara.

Chapelfield Shopping Centre
40-46 St Stephen's Street, Norwich, NR1. 01603 753344
www.chapelfield.co.uk
Over 80 stores including Ann Summers, H&M, Blooming Marvellous, River Island, House of Fraser, Jones, Oasis, Mango, French Connection, Levi's, Esprit, Monsoon, Accessorize, Republic, Warehouse and Ravel.

Gateshead Metrocentre
Metrocentre, Gateshead, Newcastle upon Tyne NE11. 0191 493 0219
www.metrocentre-gateshead.co.uk
Enormous shopping mall with branches of Accessorize, BHS, Claire's Accessories, Elvi, Fenn Wright Manson, Moda & Pelle, Mango, Paris, Principles, Ann Harvey, Bershka, Evans, Dorothy Perkins, Debenhams, H&M, Karen Millen, Laura Ashley, Marks & Spencer, Monsoon, Primark, River Island, New Look.

Gunwharf Quays
Portsmouth Harbour, Portsmouth Hampshire PO1. 02392 836700
www.gunwharf-quays.com
Designer outlet shopping centre. Shops include: Austin Reed, Burberry, Fat Face, Guess, Hobbs, Karen Millen, Whistles, Liz Claiborne, LK Bennett, Gap, Barbour CKU, Paul Smith, Ted Baker, Mexx, Reef, Next, White Stuff, and Ralph Lauren.

Junction 32
M62 Castleford West Yorkshire 01977 520153
www.junction32.com
Discount shopping centre including outlets for Lilley & Skinner, Clarks, Jane Shilton, Camille, Cotton Traders, Gossard, Ice Jeans, Oasis, Prima, Next, Monsoon, Mexx, Gap, Zara, Marks & Spencer, Lee Cooper, Liz Claiborne, Mango and The Designer Room.

Kildare Village
Nurney Road, Kildare Town, County Kildare Ireland + 353 (0) 45520501
www.kildarevillage.com
Shopping Village 30 miles outside Dublin with outlet branches of Karen Millen, Calvin Klein, Levi's, Myla, Monsoon, Coast, Pepe and LK Bennett

Lakeside Shopping Centre
West Thurrock Way, Thurrock Essex 01708 869933
www.lakeside.uk.com
Enormous shopping centre. Includes stores such as Ann Harvey, BHS, Choice Woman, Bay Trading Company, Coast, Evans, Gap, Dorothy Perkins, Debenhams, Confetti & Lace, H&M, Morgan, Marks & Spencer, Miss Selfridge, Lacoste, Jane Norman, House of Fraser, Zara, River Island, Punky Fish, Principles, The Vestry, Wallis and Warehouse.

Meadowhall
Meadowhall Centre, Sheffield, S9. 0845 600 6800
www.meadowhall.co.uk
Monster mall containing New Look, Oasis, Republic, Topshop Principles, Next, O'Neill, La Senza, Miss Selfridge, Debenhams, Ann Harvey, Coast, French Dressing, Lacoste, Jane Norman, Jacques Vert, Quiz, Wallis, House of Fraser, Warehouse, Zara, Ted Baker and many more.

The Overgate Centre
Dundee DD1. 01382 314201
www.overgate.co.uk
Located in Dundee town centre, stores include Debenhams, French Connection, Gap, H&M, La Senza, Mango, Oasis, Primark, Next, Logo, Free Spirit, Warehouse, Boots, Passion for Perfume, Office and River Island.

The Trafford Centre
Manchester M17 0161 749 1717
www.traffordcentre.co.uk
Huge upmarket shopping centre just outside Manchester city centre. Stores include: Aldo, Accessorize, Boots, BHS, Coast, Crabtree & Evelyn, Debenhams, Dune, Dorothy Perkins, Elvi, Evans, Faith, Fat Face, French Connection, Gap, Jones, Jane Norman, Karen Millen, La Senza, Mango, Molton Brown, Monsoon, Marks & Spencer, Mexx, Morgan, Miss Sixty, Next, New Look, Oasis, Office, Planet, Principles, Ravel, Reiss, Republic, River Island, Selfridges, Space.NK, Vestry, Virgin Cosmetics, Warehouse, Wallis, Wrangler and Zara.

Stockists

Wardrobe supervision: Erica Davies

Assistants: Annie Swain, Debi Simpson and Lois Strouthos

Original garments and alterations: Asuzana

THE SKITTLE
Key Shapes
Blue coat – Marni
Purple t-shirt – Zara
Grey trousers – French Connection
Brown dress – Karen Millen
Tank top – Boden
Red shirt – Kenzo at Selfridges
Brown panelled skirt – Marks & Spencer
Black jacket – Vivienne Westwood Red Label
Brown swimming costume – Melissa Odabash
Chunky heel shoes – Prada
Casual
Blue coat – Marni
Purple t-shirt – Zara
Grey trousers – French Connection
Necklace – vintage
Trainers – Converse
Smart
Brown dress – Karen Millen
Big chain necklace – vintage
Shoes – New Look
Party
Black asymmetric jacket – Vivienne Westwood Red Label
Black fishtail skirt - Zara
Shoes – Jane Shilton

THE GOBLET
Key Garments
Jeans – 7 For All Mankind at John Lewis
Purple jacket – Missoni
Tweed coat – Littlewoods
Brown top – New Look
Plum panelled skirt – Primark
Black fishtail skirt – Next
Silver knit dress – French Connection
Purple lurex knit top – Therapy at House of Fraser
Swimsuit – Miraclesuit@figleaves.com
Satin shoes – Lulu Guinness
Casual
Jeans – 7 For All Mankind at John Lewis
Brown top – New Look
Tweed coat – Littlewoods
Boots – Marks & Spencer
Smart
Purple jacket – Missoni
Purple lurex knit top – Therapy at House of Fraser
Plum panelled skirt – Primark
Satin shoes – Lulu Guinness
Party
Silver knit dress – French Connection
Brown slim heeled shoes – Christian Louboutin

THE HOURGLASS
Key Shapes
Purple t-shirt – French Connection
White shirt – Red Herring at Debenhams
Coat – trinny&susannah at Littlewoods
Dress – Tulah
Mustard jacket - Moto at Topshop
Cardigan – Marilyn Moore at Fenwick
Skirt – Jaeger
Trousers – Marks & Spencer
Necklace – vintage
Shoes – vintage
Casual
Leopard tunic – Principles
Trousers – Marks & Spencer
Necklace and shoes – vintage
Smart
White dress – Sticky Fingers at House of Fraser
Shoes – Jasper Conran for Debenhams
Ring – George at Asda
Evening
Bronze dress – Zara
Jacket – Arrogant Cat
Shoes – Luc Berjan
Earrings – vintage

THE CORNET
Key shapes
Blue stripe coat – vintage
Jeans – Zara
Wrap cardigan – Vince
Jersey dress – Issa at Zee & Co
White shirt – Dorothy Perkins
Net skirt – Diva
Cigarette pants – Day Birger & Mikkelsen
Brown striped dress – Vivienne Westwood Red Label
Red skirt – Marks & Spencer
Shoes – Office
Casual
Striped wrap jumper – All Saints
Skirt – Topshop
Tights – Falke at MyTights.com
Shoes – Olivia Morris
Smart
Coat – Vivienne Westwood
Tights – Jonathan Aston at MyTights.com
Shoes – Office
Evening
Dress – Alice Temperley
Shoes – Office vintage
Earrings – vintage

THE CELLO
Key shapes
Metallic pleated skirt – Jaeger
Black shirt – South at Littlewoods
Grey trousers – Monsoon
Pink scoop neck jumper – Belinda Robertson cashmere
Cord jacket – Gucci
Brown spotty halterneck dress – Monsoon
Gold patterned coat – trinny&susannah at Littlewoods

[continued]
Orange short-sleeved jumper – Jesire
Purple earrings – vintage
Purple wedges – Yves Saint Laurent
Casual
Grey trousers – Monsoon
Black shirt – South at Littlewoods
Blazer – Gucci
Shoes – Hobbs
Smart
Gold patterned coat – trinny&susannah at Littlewoods
Black skirt – Marks & Spencer
Silver vest – French Connection
Shoes – Christian Louboutin
Evening
Cream patterned dress – Monsoon
Shoes – Yves Saint Laurent
Earrings – vintage

THE APPLE
Key shapes
Grey top with square neckline – Autograph by Marks & Spencer
Green & yellow skirt – Monsoon
Denim jacket – Next
White shirt – Littlewoods
Duster coat – New Look
Ruched t-shirt – Zara
Floral top with band under the bust – Debenhams
Denim trousers – Monsoon
Black side zip trousers – trinny&susannah at Littlewoods
Bronze flats – Next
Gold wedges – Monsoon
Casual
Linen trousers and top – both Monsoon
Jewellery – Accessorize
Shoes – Next
Smart
White broderie-anglaise coat, grey top and grey trousers – all Marks & Spencer
Sandals – Next
Jewellery – Accessorize
Evening
Lime beaded cardigan, spotted top, skirt and gold shoes – all Monsoon

THE COLUMN
Key shapes
Green mac – Karen Millen
Yellow puff sleeve shirt – John Lewis
Rust cropped jacket – Missoni
Maroon trousers – Marks & Spencer
A-line skirt – Whistles
Round neck jumper – New Look
Necklace – vintage
Cropped trousers – Marks & Spencer
Chiffon paisley dress – Linea at House of Fraser
Nude shoes – Christian Louboutin
Casual
Green coat – Karen Millen
Green top – Jigsaw
Trousers – Asuzana
Shoes – Converse
Necklace – Vintage

Smart
Gold jacket – Allegra Hicks
Yellow linen shirt – John Lewis
Skirt – vintage
Necklace – vintage
Boots – Primark
Evening
Kimono top – Zara
Trousers – Marks & Spencer
Necklace – vintage
Shoes – Office

THE BELL
Key shapes
Striped shirt – Zara
Brown trousers – Marks & Spencer
Kaftan – Tashia
Green coat – Zara
Purple gilet – Marks & Spencer
Brown jumper – Belinda Robertson
Cashmere
Snake print shoes – Loeffler Randall
Necklace – vintage
Brown patterned coat-dress – Helene
Berman at House of Fraser
Tweed skirt – Jesire
Casual
Purple long sleeved top – Jigsaw
Purple gilet – Marks & Spencer
Purple trousers – Per Una at Marks &
Spencer
Trainers – Puma
Smart
Brown cowl neck jumper – Belinda
Robertson cashmere
Linen jacket – Zara
Trousers – Marks & Spencer
Shoes – Marks & Spencer
Evening
Purple dress – Phase Eight at John
Lewis
Necklace – vintage
Shoes – Loeffler Randall

THE VASE
Key shapes
Mustard jumper with white sleeves –
Yves Saint Laurent
Gold knit dress with scoop neck – Zara
Blue jeans – 7 For All Mankind at John
Lewis
Blue shirt – French Connection
Pencil skirt – Littlewoods
Brown trousers – trinny&susannah at
Littlewoods
Round earrings – vintage
Brown silk jacket with fastening detail –
Fenn Wright Manson at John Lewis
Red dress – Hervé Leroux
Brown shoes – Marks & Spencer
Casual
Blue/silver coat – Zara Basic
Blue shirt – French Connection
Jeans – 7 For All Mankind at John Lewis
Shoes – New Look

Smart
Cream silk shirt – Zara Basic
Brown tank top – Brora
Brown pencil skirt – Arrogant Cat
Shoes – Marks & Spencer
Evening
Dress – vintage
Shoes – Madonna for H&M

THE BRICK
Key shapes
Green jumper with beaded detail –
Principles
Blue chiffon wrap dress – All Saints
Sparkly blue skirt – The West Village
Grey skirt – Marks & Spencer
Blue 'Fuerteventura' pants – Sweaty
Betty
Black tank top – Madonna for H&M
Grey jersey top – Next
Cream coat – vintage
Shoes – Vivienne Westwood
Pinstripe jacket – vintage
Casual
Blue trousers – Sweaty Betty
Blue and cream striped cardigan – Ben
Sherman
Blue wedges – Marni
Smart
White shirt – Linea at House of Fraser
Tank top with embellishment – Marni
Skirt – Marks & Spencer
Shoes – Vivienne Westwood
Evening
Wrap dress – All Saints
Leggings – Falke at MyTights.com
Shoes – Office

THE LOLLIPOP
Key shapes
Green coat – vintage
Aztec jacket – Diane von Furstenberg
Black top – Sonia Rykiel
Trousers – Asuzana
Black skirt – Zara
Black shoes – Love Label at Littlewoods
Purple jersey skirt – Missoni
Green dress – vintage
Purple tank top – Brora
Brown bikini – Marks & Spencer
Casual
Shirt – Chloé
Trousers – Asuzana
Waistcoat – South at Littlewoods
Shoes – Marks & Spencer
Smart
Black top – Sonia Rykiel
Black skirt – Marks & Spencer
Shoes – Love Label at Littlewoods
Evening
Green dress – vintage
Shoes – Prada
Brooch – vintage

THE PEAR
Key shapes
Orange blouse – Jasper Conran for
Debenhams
Brown boots – Hobbs
Green satin platforms – Prada
Sequin bolero – vintage
Gold blazer – Whistles
Strapless dress – vintage
Long skirt – Kate Moss at Topshop
Trousers, Littlewoods
Striped jumper – Sonia Rykiel
Coat – Littlewoods
Casual
Wide leg trousers – trinny&susannah at
Littlewoods
Khaki t-shirt with fluted sleeves – French
Connection
Waistcoat – Zara
Shoes – Marks & Spencer
Smart
Lurex gold top – vintage
Gold dress – vintage
Coat – trinny&susannah at Littlewoods
Tights – Falke at MyTights.com
Chocolate brown boots – Hobbs
Evening
Dress – Monsoon
Shrug – vintage
Shoes – Office
Brooch – vintage

TRINNY AND SUSANNAH
On the cover
Trinny wears:
Purple metallic top – Asuzana
Plum skirt – Miu Miu
Necklace – vintage collection
Susannah wears:
Satin shirt – Joseph
Skirt – Zac Posen
On pages 18 and 237
Trinny wears:
Vivid green dress – Prada
Shoes – Christian Louboutin
Susannah wears:
Forest green dress – Stella McCartney
Tights – Falke at mytights.com
Shoes – Yves Saint Laurent
Inside pages:
Trinny wears:
T-shirt – Marks & Spencer (customised
by Asuzana)
Trousers – Sweaty Betty
Susannah wears:
Shirt – Joseph
Trousers – Sweaty Betty